William J. Fay

D0841373

MOSES OR JESUS
AN ESSAY IN JOHANNINE CHRISTOLOGY

MOSES OR JESUS
AN ESSAY IN JOHANNINE CHRISTOLOGY

BY

M.-É. BOISMARD

Translated by B.T. Viviano

FORTRESS PRESS
Minneapolis

PEETERS PRESS
Leuven

MOSES OR JESUS
An Essay in Johannine Christology

First North American edition published 1993 by Fortress Press.

This book is translated by B.T. Viviano from *Moïse ou Jésus: Essai de christologie johannique*, Volume 84 in the Series "Bibliotheca Ephemeridum Theologicarum Lovaniensium", © 1988 Uitgeverij Peeters & Leuven University Press, Leuven, Belgium.

English translation © 1993 by Uitgeverij Peeters, Leuven.

All rights reserved. Except for brief quotations in critical articles or reviews, no part of this book may be reproduced in any manner without prior written permission from the publisher. Write to: Permissions, Augsburg Fortress, 426 S. Fifth St., Box 1209, Minneapolis, MN 55440.

Library of Congress Cataloging-in-Publication Data

Boismard, M.-É.
    [Moïse ou Jésus. English]
    Moses or Jesus: an essay in Johannine Christology / M.-É. Boismard;
    translated by B.T. Viviano. — 1st North American ed. 144 p. 16 × 24 cm.
    Includes bibliographical references and index (p. 135-144).
    ISBN 0-8006-2751-2.
    1. Jesus Christ — History of doctrines — Early church, ca. 30-600.
    2. Bible N.T. John — Criticism, interpretation, etc. I. Title.
    BT198.B63213   1993
    232'.09'015-dc20   92-36122
                                                                            CIP

Manufactured in Belgium
97 96 95 94 93 1 2 3 4 5 6 7 8 9 10   AF 1-2751

CONTENTS

CHAPTER TWO

JESUS IS THE WISDOM OF GOD

CHAPTER THREE

THE WORD OF GOD MADE FLESH

CHAPTER FOUR

THE ONLY-BEGOTTEN

Translator's Note

The translator would like to thank the following for their collaboration in the earlier stages of the translation: Orsoline Chiappetta, Soteria Foufounis, Elizabeth Miller, Gregory F. Robison, Timothy Scott. As for quotations from the Bible, sometimes the RSV was followed, sometimes the NAB (including its 1986 revision of the New Testament). But, when the author's work of close comparison was at stake, the translation was done from his French directly, rather than using an existing English translation. The reader will notice a running debate in the section on the Three Signs between M.-É. Boismard and his devoted critic, Professor Frans Neirynck of Leuven University. For a serene and fair report on this debate, one would do well to consult Dwight Moody Smith's review article in *Biblica* 63 (1982) 102-113, and his more recent work, *John among the Gospels. The Relationship in Twentieth-Century Research*, Minneapolis, Augsburg Fortress, 1992, pp. 139-176: "The Dissolution of a Consensus" (esp. pp. 141-158).

Since the publication of the French original of this work, its author has presented an expanded and clarified version of its fourth chapter which treats of the title "son of God" in an article: "Le titre de 'fils de Dieu' dans les évangiles. Sa portée salvifique", *Biblica* 72 (1991), 442-450. The interested reader may now consult this for more details.

FOREWORD

The title of this book well defines its principal object: to understand how, in the gospel of John, Jesus realizes in his person God's
promise to send his people a prophet like Moses (Deut 18:18-19).
Jews must therefore choose between Moses and Jesus (John 9:28-
32). But this principal theme offers a certain number of harmonics.
Even if they have the same mission, to transmit the words of God,
Jesus is much superior to Moses. Moses in fact only speaks in the
name of God, as if God put his words in his mouth, to use the
biblical expression. But Jesus is the Wisdom of God made man, the
Word made flesh, the Only Begotten of God, God himself come in
person to speak to all people. Finally, although they have the same
mission, there is no common measure between Moses and Jesus. I
could not leave out these harmonics of the principal theme, but I
have treated them in a more succinct fashion.

This volume is presented as an "essay in Johannine Christology".
That means that it is not a complete Johannine Christology. I have
treated only those themes which directly make up the harmonics of
our principal theme. The role of Wisdom or of the Word is situated
in the same line as Moses: to transmit the expression of the divine
will to humanity. But, *in itself*, the eschatological title "Son of man",
for example, taking up Daniel 7:13, has nothing to do with the
prophetic theme; we have therefore not said anything about it.

For a long time now a number of exegetes have seen Samaritan
influences on the redaction of John's gospel. Now the text of Deut
18:18-19, announcing the coming of a prophet like Moses, held a
great place in Samaritan thought. I was therefore led to study rather
closely to what extent the gospel of John depended on Samaritan
tradition. I believe I have brought forward a certain number of new
arguments, rather decisive ones at that, which permit us to answer
the question in the affirmative.

From the outset of my work, I had to make a choice. In 1977, I
had published, in collaboration with Arnaud Lamouille, a commentary on the gospel of John in which we distinguished four successive
redactional levels[1]. Should I take this distinction into account in

1. M.-É. Boismard and A. Lamouille, *L'évangile de Jean* (Synopse des quatre évangiles

working out the analyses of the present volume? But that would at the same time draw criticism from those who do not share these views. I have therefore preferred to treat the problem by taking the gospel of John as it presents itself to us, from a synchronic angle. I have made only one exception, which proved to be indispensable, when I developed the theme of the three miracles worked by Jesus in Galilee, miracles intended to prove the authenticity of his mission, like the miracles which Moses performed at God's order according to Exod 4: 1-9. But in this case, I have simply spoken of a source used by the evangelist, a conclusion which would not disturb most exegetes, and which would, in part only, fit the view of Bultmann and those who have followed him in his reconstruction of the Signs-Source (*Semeia-Quelle*). In general therefore, I will speak of "the gospel of John" or even of "John", thereby abstracting from the problems of literary criticism which relate to the fourth gospel.

It was however interesting to ask whether Johannine Christology had not undergone an evolution. I could not do it except in function of the analyses worked out in the third volume of our Synopsis. The reader will find a brief presentation in the last chapter of the present work, a chapter we could entitle: from the Prophet like Moses to God incarnate. There we will see the realization of this statement attributed to Jesus by the evangelist: "I have much more to tell you, but you cannot bear it now. But when he comes, the Spirit of truth, he will guide you to all truth" (John 16: 12-13).

In his *Theology of the New Testament*, Rudolf Bultmann has devoted almost 100 pages to the Johannine writings, gospel and letters[2]. Surprisingly we find there hardly any reference to Old Testament texts. For Bultmann, Johannine thought is explainable almost entirely on the basis of the Gnostic Hellenistic myth of the Redeemer, sent into the world as Revealer of the divine mysteries. One has the impression that, for Bultmann, John ignored just about everything in the Old Testament, except for a few references to the great figures of Abraham and Moses (John 5: 45-47; 8: 56-58). From this viewpoint, my interpretation of Johannine thought is at the

---

en français, tome III), Paris, 1977. We will cite this volume under the title *Synopse III*. It was intended for a wide public and therefore not provided with any scholarly apparatus. We will here take up some of the analyses which are found in it, but give them a more systematic and technical exposition.

2. R. Bultmann, *Theologie des Neuen Testaments*, Tübingen, 3rd edition 1958, pp. 354-445.

opposite pole from that of Bultmann: the Johannine Christ is situated above all in the line of the prophets, and especially of Moses, who were sent by God to reveal his will to men. My reaction then rejoins that of Juan Peter Miranda who, in a Tübingen Catholic Faculty dissertation[3], has well shown that the theme of the sending of the Christ by God derived from the Old Testament (prophetic and wisdom traditions) and not from Gnostic thought. My analyses will often overlap with his. I should also refer to Günter Reim's book concerning the Old Testament background of John's gospel[4], especially the chapter in which he analyses the theme of Jesus, the prophet like Moses (pp. 110ff).

I have filled out the French edition of this short book by adding, as an appendix, three articles which had appeared either in the *Revue Biblique* or in *Lumière et Vie*[5]. They are relevant to some of the themes treated here. They are not translated in the English edition but references are given here for the interested reader. The first article, entitled "Aenon, près de Salem (Jean, iii, 23)", appeared in *RB* 80 (1973) 218-229; it sheds light on the problem of the Samaritan origin of the fourth gospel. The second complementary article entitled "Une liturgie baptismale dans la *Prima Petri*", which appeared in *RB* 63 (1956) 182-208 and 64 (1957) 161-183[6], develops the theme of our new birth from the Word of God, which I only touch upon on pages 92f of the present volume. This theme has moreover as its background a whole baptismal typology of the Exodus which links up with our basic theme of Jesus as new Moses. This baptismal typology of the Exodus is again found in the well known formula "Je renonce à Satan et à ses œuvres", as we have shown in an article of the same title which appeared in *Lumière et Vie* 26 (1956) 105-110.

---

3. J.P. Miranda, *Der Vater, der mich gesandt hat. Religionsgeschichtliche Untersuchungen zu den johanneischen Sendungsformeln. Zugleich ein Beitrag zur johanneischen Christologie und Ekklesiologie* (Europäische Hochschulschriften, 23/7), Bern-Frankfort, 1972. See also by the same author, *Die Sendung Jesu im vierten Evangelien. Religions- und theologie-geschichtliche Untersuchungen zu den Sendungsformeln* (Stuttgarter Bibelstudien, 87), Stuttgart, 1977.

4. G. Reim, *Studien zum alttestamentlichen Hintergrund des Johannesevangeliums* (SNTS Monograph Series, 22), Cambridge, 1974.

5. *Moïse ou Jésus*, pp. 145-158 (I), 159-216 (II), 217-222 (III).

6. These articles were in part taken up and developed in my book entitled *Quatre hymnes baptismales dans la première épître de Pierre* (Lectio Divina, 30), Paris, 1961.

At the close of this Foreword I would like to thank my confrère Arnaud Lamouille who helped with the indices and proofs. I would also like to thank Professor Frans Neirynck and Leuven University for the conferral of an honorary doctorate and the acceptance of the original edition of this book in their collection BETL.

Jerusalem 1988

CHAPTER ONE

JESUS, THE PROPHET LIKE MOSES

In Deut 18:18-19, God declares to Moses, in speaking about the Hebrews: "I will raise up for them, from the midst of their kinsmen, a prophet like you: I will put my words in his mouth and he will say to them everything that I will command him to say. If a man does not listen to my words which this prophet will have pronounced in my name, I myself will call him to account". God will thus raise up for his people, at some future date, a prophet like Moses who will have for a mission to transmit to men and women His own words. The people in turn must obey everything the prophet will say in God's name; for them it is a question of life or death. This text took on considerable importance in the Jewish and Samaritan tradition. But, while it is not unknown in the synoptic tradition, it holds an essential place in the gospel of John since it governs most of its Christology. We will briefly overview the use of Deut 18:18-19 in the Hebrew Scriptures and in Qumran, as well as in the Samaritan tradition. Then, we will analyse how it was systematically used in the fourth gospel. This study of Johannine Christology will in turn lead us to delve again into the Samaritan traditions.

I. JEWISH AND SAMARITAN TRADITIONS

The text which most interests us is the call of Jeremiah, for we will find the same literary devices in the Gospel of John.

1. *The Call of Jeremiah (Jer 1:5-10)*

At the beginning of his oracles, the prophet Jeremiah tells how he was called by God to carry His words against the pagan nations. The literary contact between Jer 1:7-9 and Deut 18:18 is certain:

Deut 18:18	ונתתי דברי בפיו ודבר אליהם את כל אשר אצונו
Jer 1:9, 7	הנה נתתי דברי בפיך/ואת כל אשר אצוק תדבר
Deut 18:18	and I will put my words in his mouth and he will say everything that I will command him to say
Jer 1:9	look how I will put my words in your mouth
Jer 1:7	and everything which I will command, you will say

In which direction did the literary borrowing occur? Holladay[1], who has studied these texts in detail, has clearly shown that the chronology of Jeremiah must be corrected, and that the text in question depends on Deut 18:18. This conclusion is confirmed by the fact that Jer 1:5ff demonstrates thematic contacts with the stories of the call of Moses. In Jer 1:6, the prophet wants to refuse his role: "I cannot speak, as I am young". Likewise in Exod 4:10, Moses objects to his mission: "I am not a man of words... because my mouth is heavy and my tongue is heavy". In Jer 1:7-8, God speaks to the prophet: "You will go to those to whom *I will send you...* Have no fear before them, for *I am with you* to deliver you". Likewise, God had spoken to Moses: "Go, *I send you* to Pharaoh... *I will be with you* and here is the sign which will show you that *I have sent you*". It is thus Jeremiah who depends on the texts concerning Moses.

The parallel between Jeremiah and Moses is also found in other passages. For example, Jeremiah records in a particular way a command from God: "Take another scroll and write on it all the words, the first ones, which were on the first scroll burned by Jehoiakim, King of Judah" (Jer 36:28); the allusion is clearly to Exod 34:1, the words addressed to Moses: "Cut for yourself two tables of stone like the first ones and I will write on the tables the words which were on the first tables which you have broken". Jeremiah wishes to indicate that he too received an order analogous to the one received by Moses after he had broken the tables of the Law. One could cite other similar instances[2].

Therefore, Jeremiah is conscious of accomplishing in his person the promise made by God in Deut 18:18 to send to his people a prophet like Moses. He is himself the awaited prophet, which he underlines by appropriating the language of Deut 18:18 as a description of his own vocation. He further attributes to himself the words and the context found in the Pentateuch for Moses. It is

---

1. William L. Holladay, "The Background of Jeremiah's Self-Understanding: Moses, Samuel, and Psalm 22", *JBL* 83 (1965) 153-164; "Jeremiah and Moses: Further Observations", *JBL* 85 (1966) 17-27. This theme had already been treated by P.E. Broughton, "The Call of Jeremiah. The Relation of Deut 18:9-22 to the Call of Jeremiah", *Australian Biblical Review* 6 (1958) 37-46. See also Norman Habel, "The Form and Significance of the Call Narratives", *ZAW* 77 (1965) 297-323, esp. p. 306.

2. See Luis Alonso Schökel, "Jeremias como anti-Moisés", in *De la Tôrah au Messie. Mélanges Henri Cazelles*, 1981, pp. 245-254.

precisely this literary structure which recurs in the gospel of John to demonstrate that Jesus is the prophet like Moses predicted in Deut 18:18. Before describing this, let us briefly examine the importance of this text of Deuteronomy for subsequent Jewish and Samaritan reflection at the time of the NT.

2. *Deut 18:18-19 at Qumran*

It is difficult to determine to what extend the Qumran community accorded this text a particular importance. A fragment from cave 4 (4Q158,6)[3] gives in sequence: Exod 20:19-22; Deut 5:29; Deut 18:18-20, 22. But J. Strugnell[4] suggests: "This fragment... is in fact almost entirely the *Samaritan* text of Exodus 20:19-21b, with all its composite characteristics clearly identifiable". M. Baillet arrived at the same conclusion in a detailed study of the Samaritan text of Exodus. Concerning this fragment he writes: "In reality, this follows the Samaritan text"[5]. The same must be said for fragment 4Q175, which includes Deut 5:28-29; Exod 20:21; Deut 18:18-19; Num 24:15-17; Deut 33:8-11 and Jos 6:26[6].

Thus we find ourselves confronted by a larger problem; what was the relationship between the Qumran sect and the Samaritans? Later on, we will make clear that this question does not directly concern us in this study. It is moreover clear that within the literature which finds its origin at Qumran, this text, Deut 18:18-19, did not have a special place. We know that the Qumran sectarians awaited two messiahs, one a warrior, the other a priest, and that their coming would be preceded by a prophet; but nothing indicates that this indeterminate prophet should be identified with the prophet like Moses of Deut 18:18-19.

3. *Deut 18:18-19 and the Samaritans*

Two Samaritan texts identify explicitly the Taheb with the prophet like Moses announced in Deut 18, but they are rather late; a 14th century Samaritan author and a 17th century liturgical hymn. On the other hand, in the earliest extant Samaritan text, the *Memar Marqah*,

---

3. Published by J. Allegro, in *Qumran Cave 4, I (4Q158-4Q186)* (DJD V), 1968, p. 3.
4. John Strugnell, "Notes en marge du vol. V des Discoveries in the Judaean Desert of Jordan", *Revue de Qumran* 7 (1970) 225.
5. M. Baillet, "Le texte samaritain de l'Exode dans les manuscrits de Qumrân", in *Hommages à André Dupont-Sommer*, 1971, p. 367.
6. Published by John Allegro, pp. 57-60.

which dates from the fourth century, there is no relation between the Taheb and Deut 18. Furthermore, Marqah frequently suggests that there will never be another prophet as great as Moses. According to Kippenberg[7], the Samaritan Taheb would never have been linked to the promises of Deut 18. Dexinger[8] opposed this view in taking up the question using other criteria. We will see later to what extent our analysis of the fourth Gospel can be of use in resolving the question. Recall for the moment one sure fact: from the first century B.C., as is proven by the Qumran texts, the Samaritans gave prominence to Deut 18, because they repeated it in their recension of the Pentateuch. In one case it is found in its normal place in the text; the second time it is found after Exod 20:21, at the conclusion of the episode where the Law is given through the intermediary of Moses. We know as well that the Samaritans kept only the Pentateuch as inspired Scripture; therefore they had to depend on the Pentateuch alone as a basis for their eschatological hopes. The text of Deut 18 then found a significant place in their consciousness. We shall see that the Gospel of John, in portraying Jesus as the Prophet predicted in Deut 18, is closely dependent on the Samaritan traditions.

II. THE GOSPEL OF JOHN

The problem of a possible influence of Samaritan traditions on the gospel of John was posed in systematic fashion in 1958 by John Bowman, in an article which had a considerable impact[9]. For him, the contact point between the gospel of John and Samaritan theology would be the fact that it attributes to the pre-existant Christ what Samaritan theology attributes to the pre-existent Moses (p. 308). We could think that, by writing his gosple, John would have wanted to build a bridge between Samaritans and Jews, in Christ. — Independently of Bowman's article, Wayne A. Meeks, in 1967[10], also thought

7. H.G. Kippenberg, *Garizim und Synagoge* (Religionsgeschichtliche Versuche und Vorarbeiten 30), Berlin, de Gruyter, 1971, pp. 304-312.

8. F. Dexinger, "Der 'Prophet wie Mose' in Qumran und bei den Samaritanern", in *Mélanges bibliques et orientaux en l'honneur de Mathias Delcor* (AOAT 215), 1985, 97-111.

9. J. Bowman, "Samaritan Studies. I: The Fourth Gospel and the Samaritans", *BJRL* 40 (1958) 298-308.

10. W.A. Meeks, *The Prophet-King. Moses Traditions and the Johannine Christology* (Supp. to NT, 14), 1967 (esp. pp. 250-254).

of a Samaritan theological influence on the Johannine way of conceiving Jesus as prophet and king. — A year later, E.D. Freed picked up and developed Bowman's article by drawing attention to the main localizations proper to the gospel of John[11]. He also took up and sharpened the arguments brought out by Meeks. — In the same year an article by G.W. Buchanan appeared[12]. It was more radical but also more debatable than that of Bowman. He noted the importance of the term "Israel" in the gospel of John. He suggested that the title "son of Joseph" attributed to Jesus (John 1:45) had a double meaning and referred implicitly to the patriarch Joseph, the ancestor of the Samaritans. He thought that the anti-Jewish polemic of the fourth gospel reflected in fact a Samaritan polemic against the Judeans. He concluded tht the fourth gospel had a Christo-Samaritan origin. — In 1970, Freed wrote a second article[13] to advance new arguments for the thesis of Bowman and Meeks. But, more nuanced, he concluded that John wrote, not to build a bridge between Samaritans and Jews, but to set forth Christianity in such a way as to elicit conversions from both Samaritans and Jews. — Two years later appeared an article by C.H.H. Scobie[14] which, in part, treated a possible influence of Samaritan thought on the gospel of John. Without adducing new arguments, he viewed with favor the works we have surveyed.

But a reaction in the opposite direction was inevitable. In 1975, J.D. Purvis[15] criticized a certain number of arguments advanced to establish the influence of Samaritan thought on the gospel of John. While recognizing the importance of the Moses theme in the two traditions, he rejected the idea of a gospel written to attract Samaritans to the Christian faith. Quite to the contrary, the fourth gospel underlines how much Jesus is at once like Moses and different from Moses; he wants thereby to show that Jesus is superior to Moses. — But the most radical reaction was that of M. Pamment, in 1982[16]. For her, there

11. E.D. Freed, "Samaritan Influence in the Gospel of John", *CBQ* 30 (1968) 580-587.

12. G.W. Buchanan, "The Samaritan Origin of the Gospel of John", in *Religions in Antiquity. Essays in Memory of Erwin Ramsdell Goodenough*, ed. by Jacob Neusner (Studies in the History of Religions, 14), 1968.

13. E.D. Freed, "Did John Write his Gospel partly to win Samaritan Converts?", *NovT* 12 (1970) 241-256.

14. C.H.H. Scobie, "The Origins and Development of Samaritan Christianity", *NTS* 19 (1972-73) 390-414, esp. 401-408.

15. J.D. Purvis, "The Fourth Gospel and the Samaritans", *NovT* 17 (1975) 161-198.

16. M. Pamment, "Is There Convincing Evidence of Samaritan Influence on the Fourth Gospel?", *ZNW* 73 (1982) 221-230.

would be no direct contact between Samaritan thought and the gospel of John. The similarity of certain themes in the two traditions would derive from an analogous use of the Septuagint.

We do not intend, in this chapter, to re-examine the arguments advanced to establish an influence of Samaritan thought on the gospel of John. We are simply going to present some new arguments to show, on the one hand the importance in the fourth gospel of the theme of Jesus new Moses[17]; on the other hand the insertion of this theme in Samaritan thought.

A. *Jesus is "The Prophet"*

Three times, in the gospel of John, Jesus is called "the Prophet" (ὁ προφήτης). He is not only "a prophet", who would fit in the line of the Old Testament prophets[18], he is "the Prophet" par excellence. What is the range of this title?

1. *Two Parallel Titles: "the Christ" and "the Prophet"*

Let us first note that, in a more or less formal manner, it occurs parallel with another title: "the Christ".

a) This parallelism is obvious in 7:40-41, where we have these two successive confessions of faith:

οὗτός ἐστιν ἀληθῶς ὁ προφήτης	This is truly the Prophet
οὗτός ἐστιν ὁ Χριστός	This is the Christ

b) The second text, in 7:52, is closely linked to the first. It forms the conclusion of the episode begun in 7:40-41, verses whose themes and in part whose expressions it takes up. To understand it better, let us set the texts before us:

7:40-42	7:52
	ἐραύνησον καὶ ἴδε
οὗτός ἐστιν ἀληθῶς ὁ προφήτης	ὅτι [ὁ] προφήτης
οὗτός ἐστιν ὁ Χριστός...	

---

17. Other NT writings presented Jesus as the prophet like Moses foretold in Deut 18:18. This text is explicitly cited in regard to Jesus in Acts 3:22-23 (cf. 7:37). For the Synoptics, esp. Matthew, see Howard M. Teeple, *The Mosaic Eschatological Prophet* (SBL Monograph Series 10), 1957, esp. pp. 74ff.

18. Cf. Matt 14:5; 16:14; 21:26, 46; Mark 6:15; Luke 7:16; 9:19; 24:19.

μὴ γὰρ
ἐκ τῆς Γαλιλαίας   ἐκ τῆς Γαλιλαίας
ὁ Χριστὸς ἔρχεται;   οὐκ ἐγείρεται
οὐχ ἡ γραφὴ εἶπεν ὅτι... ἀπὸ
Βηθλέεμ τῆς κώμης ὅπου ἦν Δαυὶδ
ὁ Χριστὸς ἔρχεται;

                                          search and see that

this is truly the Prophet   [the] Prophet
this is the Christ
is it that, in fact,
the Christ comes from Galilee?   does not arise from Galilee
does not Scripture say that...
it is from Bethlehem, the village where
David was, that the Christ comes?

The text of 7:52 sets us first a text-critical problem[19]. The article before the noun "prophet" is only attested by P[66], the earliest witness here of the Johannine text, and by the Sahidic Coptic version (the other versions are neutral because they cannot express the definite article)[20]. Despite the fewness of the witnesses in its favor, we should prefer this reading with the article, as a comparison with 7:40-41 will show. In this last text, we have just seen, there are two parallel formulae: "This is truly the Prophet" and "This is the Christ". Now we have an analogous parallelism between 7:41 and 7:52: "Does the Christ come from Galilee?" and "[the] Prophet does not come from Galilee". It is clear then that, in 7:52, the term "prophet" ought to have the article as in 7:40. Moreover, we should note the verb "to search" (ἐραυνᾶν) with which the text of 7:52 begins. It occurs only six times in the NT, two of these in the gospel of John: here and in 5:39. In the latter text, it possesses a direct object: "You search the Scriptures...". If we relate 7:52 first with 5:39, then with 7:40-42, we see that the imperative of 7:52 "Search" means in fact "Search the Scriptures". In these conditions, how could the Jews say to Nicodemus: "Search (the Scriptures) and see that *a* prophet does not arise in Galilee"? Many prophets came from the Northern Kingdom, and more precisely, 2 Kings 14:25 explicitly says that the prophet Jonah, son of Amittai, was from Gath-Hepher, a town located in Galilee, west of Tiberias. The text of 7:52 is better understood if it is a matter, not of a prophet like the others, but

19. Cf. J. Mehlmann, "Propheta a Moyse Promissus in Jo 7,52 citatus", *VD* 44 (1966) 79-88. He concludes that the article is authentic.

20. Bodmer Papyrus XV (P[75]) has a lacuna of some letters at this place. The editors of this papyrus reconstructed the text by adding the article in front of "prophet", given the width of the lacuna, but this reconstruction has been challenged, rightly it seems.

of the Prophet par excellence. Since no OT text treats the origin of this Prophet, we must conclude that there was a transference of the theme of the Judean origin of the Christ, according to Micah 5:1 (7:41-42), to "the Prophet" spoken of in 7:40 and 7:52. This transference would have been impossible if it had been a matter of any prophet whatsoever, and not of the Prophet par excellence who, in 7:40-41, is put parallel with "the Christ"[21].

c) In 6:14, we read a confession of faith analogous to that of 7:40, a bit more developed. It is isolated here, but we should compare it with the confession of faith which Martha makes in 11:27, which has a similar structure:

6:14 οὗτός ἐστιν ἀληθῶς ὁ προφήτης ὁ ἐρχόμενος εἰς τὸν κόσμον
11:27 σὺ εἶ ὁ Χριστὸς ὁ υἱὸς τοῦ θεοῦ ὁ εἰς τὸν κόσμον ἐρχόμενος

6:14 he is truly the Prophet who comes into the world
11:27 you are the Christ, the Son of God, who comes into the world

Here, the titles "the Prophet" and "the Christ" are determined by the same formula which is not found elsewhere in the gospel of John, which confirms their equivalence.

d) We must still mention 1:21-22, with its negative formula in regard to John the Baptist: "I am not *the Christ*... Are you Elijah? I am not. Are you *the Prophet*? No". Despite the insertion of the person Elijah, there is definitely a parallelism here between "the Christ" and "the Prophet".

2. The Meaning of the Title "the Christ"

Since the two titles "the Prophet" and "the Christ" are here parallel, there must be some equivalence between them. Better to understand the range of the title "the Prophet" we must first rapidly sketch the meaning of the title "the Christ".

In Hebrew, the verb משׁח means "to anoint, to smear with oil". For the passive participle, there is the form משׁיח, "anointed". A Greek *transcription* of this participle gives the term μεσσίας, whence the English "Messiah" (John 1:41; 4:25). But a translation of the same participle gives us the term Χριστός, whence the English "Christ". The

21. We have a dubious analogue in 1:45-46. We will see that, in 1:45, the expression "the one about whom Moses wrote in the Law" refers to Deut 18:18, and points therefore implicitly to the Prophet like Moses. It is precisely about him that Nathanael asks: "Can something good come out of Nazareth?".

Christ, or the Messiah, is thus someone who has received an anointing with oil, almost always from God who destines him to fulfill a specific function. Sometimes it is a matter of the prophetic office (1 Kings 19:16; cf. Ps 105:15). Elsewhere, it is Cyrus who is anointed by God to liberate his people (Isa 45:1). But most often, anointing is the rite by which the king whom God has chosen for Israel is consecrated. This theme is already expressed in Judges 9:8, in the apologue of the trees in search of a king: "One day the trees went out *to anoint a king* to reign over them...". The first king of Israel was Saul; now Samuel received this order from God in his regard: "The time has come, I will send you a man of the tribe of Benjamin; you will anoint him as leader over my people Israel" (1 Sam 9:16; cf. 10:1, 16). Saul had David as his successor, of whom it is said: "The men of Juda came, and there they anointed David as king over the house of Juda" (2 Sam 2:4; cf. 5:3 and 1 Sam 16:1-13). Afterwards, all the other kings had to be consecrated by the anointing with oil: but the king par excellence remained David, the type of all the kings of Israel (2 Sam 7:12-16).

Later on, the adjective "anointed" became a noun to refer to the king himself; he is "the Anointed" par excellence, the "Christ". We read for example in 2 Sam 19:22, in reference to David: "Does not Shimei deserve death for having cursed the Anointed of Yahweh?" (τὸν Χριστὸν κυρίου). Similarly, Ps 2:2 speaks of poeple who "have rebelled against Yahweh and against his Anointed" (κατὰ τὸν Χριστὸν αὐτοῦ), and according to v. 6, we see that the one anointed by God is none other than the king of Israel: "It is I who have set my king over Zion...". The very title "Christ" implies therefore that of "King".

This equivalence is admitted by the authors of the NT. It is sufficient to mention the text of John 7:41-42 already quoted: "Others said: He is the Christ. But others said: Can the Christ come from Galilee? Does not Scripture say that it is of David's race, and from Bethlehem, the village where David was, that the Christ comes?".

3. *Meaning of the Title "the Prophet"*

We have already seen that, in the fourth gospel, the two titles "the Prophet" and "the Christ" were put in parallel; they must then have an analogous range. Just as therefore the Christ is the one who must come into the world (11:27) because he was announced by the Scriptures, so too the Prophet is the one who must come into the world (6:14) because he was announced by the Scriptures. But in the Bible (i.e., the

Old Testament), only one text announces the sending in the future of a particular prophet: it is Deut 18:18-19. We may therefore think that, for the author of the fourth gospel, if Jesus is "the prophet" par excellence, it is with reference to this oracle of Deuteronomy.

We have a confirmation of this in 6:14-15. Jesus has just performed the miracle of the multiplication of the loaves, which makes the enthusiastic crowd say: "This one is truly the Prophet who comes into the world", and they want to carry him off to make him king. But this miracle of the multiplication of the loaves should call to mind, not only the precedent of the prophet Elijah (2 Kings 4:42-44), but also that of Moses feeding the Hebrews in the desert. The whole discourse which is going to follow plays indeed on the antithetic parallelism which exists, in regard to the manna, between Jesus and Moses (6:30ff). There can be no doubt then that, in 6:14, the expression "the Prophet who comes into the world" alludes to the prophet like Moses announced in Deut 18:18-19.

B. *Implicit Quotations*

To show that Jesus can be compared to this or to that figure of the Old Testament, there is a literary procedure frequently used by the New Testament authors: they make up a biblical text concerning the person in question and they use it more or less literally in regard to Jesus. This is what we could call the "imitative style". Sometimes the Old Testament allusion is quite clear; it is a real quotation, even if it is not presented explicitly as such. Thus, in the story of the raising of the widow's son of Nain (Luke 7:11-17), two traits recall the story of the raising of the widow's son of Sarephtha by Elijah: the fact that it is the only son of a widow, and especially the conclusion which we read in v. 15 of the Lucan account: "And he handed him over to his mother". This sentence is taken over textually from 1 Kings 17:23. Luke thereby wants to suggest that Jesus is a prophet who can be compared to Elijah, whence the reaction of the bystanders: "A great prophet has risen among us". Similarly, in John 2:5, at the wedding feast of Cana, Mary says to the servants about Jesus: "All that he tells you to do, do it". This is, quite literally, the sentence which Pharaoh spoke to the Egyptians about Joseph, at the beginning of the great famine which threatened to ravage the country (Gen 41:55). This implicit quotation indicates to us that Jesus should be compared to the patriarch Joseph.

These two cases are quite clear, because the quotations are almost literal. But often, the allusion to Old Testament texts will only consist in the use of common themes, with some related vocabulary. This literary procedure was widely used by the author, or the authors, of the fourth gospel to show that Jesus was this prophet like Moses announced in Deut 18:18-19. In this they only, as we noted above, followed the example of Jeremiah who wanted to compare himself to Moses. This is what we are now going to show.

1. *John 12:48-50*

The editing of these sayings attributed to Jesus is without any doubt inspired by the text of Deut 18:18-19 concerning the sending of a prophet like Moses. But to understand it better it is necessary to underline the differences between the Hebrew text and its Greek translation by the Septuagint.

a) Deut 18:18-19

נביא אקים להם מקרב אחיהם כמוך

תתתי דברי בפיו

ודבר אליהם את כל אשר אצונו

והיה האיש אשר לא ישמע אל דברי אשר ידבר בשמי

אנכי אדרש מעמו

"A prophet I will raise up for them, from the midst of your brethren, like you; and I will put my words in his mouth, and he shall say to them all that I command him. And whoever will not give heed to my words which he will say in my name, I myself will require it of him".

προφήτην ἀναστήσω αὐτοῖς ἐκ τῶν ἀδελφῶν αὐτῶν ὥσπερ σὲ
καὶ δώσω τὸ ῥῆμά μου ἐν τῷ στόματι αὐτοῦ
καὶ λαλήσει αὐτοῖς καθότι ἂν ἐντείλωμαι αὐτῷ
καὶ ὁ ἄνθρωπος ὃς ἐὰν μὴ ἀκούσῃ ὅσα ἐὰν λαλήσῃ ὁ προφήτης ἐπὶ τῷ
ὀνόματί μου ἐγὼ ἐκδικήσω ἐξ αὐτοῦ

"A prophet I will raise up for them from their brothers, like you, and I will give my word in his mouth; and he shall speak to them as I will have commanded him; and the man who will not listen to whatever the prophet shall speak in my name, I will take vengeance on him".

The Septuagint translated this text quite literally. Let us however note some details of its translation. In these two verses it has translated the Hebrew verb דבר in the piel, not by λέγειν, but by λαλεῖν (the difference between *dire* and *parler* in French, between *say* and *speak* in English). — In v. 18, we translated the Hebrew ונתתי by "and I will put". But the verb נתן means "put" or "place" as well as "give"; whence the translation of the Septuagint, less correct: δώσω ("and I will give"). — In the same verse, after the expression "and he will say to them", the Hebrew text offers a direct object governed by the preposition אֵת. But the Septuagint introduced a conjunction indicating the comparison: "and he will speak to them *as* (καθότι ἄν) I will command him". — In v. 19, the Septuagint made explicit the subject of the verb "to speak" by adding the noun "the prophet".

The meaning of the passage is not difficult. We note only two points. In v. 18, the formula "I will put my words in his mouth" expresses a rather current theme in the prophetic literature to mean that the prophet only respeaks the very words of God (cf. Jer 1:9; Isa 59:21). On the other hand, the idea that the prophet says what God *commands him* is only read elsewhere in the Bible in Jer 1:7 which, as we have already seen, depends on Deut 18:18.

b) John 12:48-50

48 ὁ ἀθετῶν ἐμὲ καὶ μὴ λαμβάνων τὰ ῥήματά μου ἔχει τὸν κρινόντα
    αὐτόν. ὁ λόγος ὃν ἐλάλησα ἐκεῖνος κρινεῖ αὐτὸν ἐν τῇ ἐσχάτῃ
    ἡμέρᾳ.
49 A ὅτι ἐγὼ ἐξ ἐμαυτοῦ οὐκ ἐλάλησα
    B   ἀλλ' ὁ πέμψας με πατὴρ αὐτός μοι ἐντολὴν δέδωκεν
    C   τί εἴπω καὶ τί λαλήσω
50 D   καὶ οἶδα ὅτι ἡ ἐντολὴ αὐτοῦ ζωὴ αἰώνιός ἐστιν.
    C'   ἃ οὖν ἐγὼ λαλῶ
    B'   καθὼς εἴρηκέν μοι ὁ πατὴρ
    A' οὕτως λαλῶ

48 He who rejects me and does not receive my sayings has a judge; the
    word that I have spoken will be his judge on the last day.
49 A For I have not spoken on my own (authority);
    B but the Father who sent me has himself given me commandment
    C   what to say and what to speak.
50 D   and I know that this commandment is eternal life.
    C'   What I speak, therefore,
    B' as the Father has bidden me
    A' I speak.

Here too, we have translated the Greek λαλεῖν by the verb "to speak", even if the result is bad English, in order to distinguish it from λέγειν (to say). The construction as a chiasm of v. 49-50 is obvious, with at the center the theme of eternal life. We refind, in this Johannine text, the two main themes of Deut 18:18-19, but inverted: the Prophet speaks the words which God *orders him* to speak; whoever does not listen to these words will be punished. Let us take up these two themes again in the order in which they are read in Deut 18:18-19.

It is remarkable to note that the two parallel sentences which are read in v. 49b and 50b of the Johannine text correspond in part, the first to the Hebrew text of Deut 18:19, the second to the Septuagint translation thereof:

TM   and *he will say to them* everything *which* I will command him
Jn 49 He commanded me *what I should say*
Jn 50 *as* the Father spoke to me, so *I speak*
LXX   *he will speak* to them *as* I have commanded him

At v. 49, we have the verb "to say" followed by a direct complement, as in the TM; but at v. 50, it is the verb "to speak" followed by a conjunction indicating a comparison. This fact cannot be attributed to chance. The Johannine text follows both the Hebrew text (or that of a targum, cf. below) and that of the Septuagint. This duality could explain the curious redundance which we notice in v. 49b: "... what I will say (Hebrew) and what I will speak (Septuagint)".

V. 48 of the Johannine text offers the same theme as Deut 18:19: whoever does not accept the words of Jesus will be condemned. Here again, we must make some precisions. We have seen in regard to v. 49b that the reference to Deut 18:18 can be made either according to the Hebrew text or according to a targum. Now, at the end of Deut 18:19, we read in Targum Neofiti: "... I, *by my Word*, will take vengeance on him". Targum Pseudo-Jonathan offers an analogous text: "... my Word will take vengeance on him". It is thus the Word which must punish the one who will not listen to the word of the Prophet like Moses. This is also what the text of John says: "... *the word* which I have spoken, it will judge him on the last day". Another detail of the text of John 12:48 turns our attention to the targums. In place of "the man who does *not listen to* the words", we read "whoever does *not receive* my words". Now the Aramaic verb קבל in the piel means especially "to receive", but also "to listen to" or "to obey". We can also note that, in Deut 18:19, to render the Hebrew שמע, Targum Neofiti has the same verb while Targum Pseudo-Jonathan has the verb קבל in the piel. In all likelihood, John's v. 49 could be referring to a targumic text such as: "And the man who does not receive the words which (the Prophet) will have pronounced in my name, my Word will take vengeance on him" (or else: "I, by my Word, will take vengeance on him").

We can thus conclude by affirming that, in John 12:48-50, Jesus takes to his account, as Jeremiah had done, the saying of Deut 18:18-19 concerning the Prophet like Moses whom God would send to his people. The reference to this text is made both according to a targum and according to the Septuagint.

The beginning of v. 49 has no parallel in Deut 18:18-19: "...because I have *not* spoken *of myself*, but the Father *who sent me*...". The words which we have underlined refer to Num 16:28: "Hereby you shall know that God *has sent me* to do all these works, and that it has *not been of my own accord*". We will take up this problem in connection with the following text.

We read in John 12:50a, at the center of the chiasm: "And I know that his commandment is eternal life". We obtain eternal life by keeping the commandments of God. This idea is frequently expressed in the Bible, and especially in the Pentateuch. But the Johannine formulation is especially close to Deut 11:8, a text in which Moses exhorts the Hebrews in these terms: "And you shall keep all his commandments... that you may live".

2. *John 8: 28-29*

When you have lifted up the Son of man, then you will know that I am he, and that I do nothing on my own authority but speak thus as the Father taught me. And the Father who sent me is with me; he has not left me alone, for I always do what is pleasing to him.

This text is woven out of biblical reminiscence. The most important one comes from Num 16:28, which we shall analyse first, by noting how the two partially parallel texts John 8:28-29 and John 12:49-50 (see above) depend upon it.

a) Num 16:28

בזאת תדעון כי יהוה שלחני לעשות את כל המעשים האלה כי לא מלבי

ἐν τούτῳ γνώσεσθε ὅτι κύριος ἀπέστειλέν με ποιῆσαι πάντα τὰ ἔργα ταῦτα, ὅτι οὐκ ἀπ᾽ ἐμαυτοῦ

by this *you shall know* that the Lord *has sent me to do* all *these* works; that *not of myself*

The text of the Septuagint translates without variant the Hebrew text. The context is the revolt of Korah, Dathan and Abiram against

Moses. They reproach him for having raised himself up as head above all the people: "Why then do you exalt yourselves above the assembly of the Lord?" (16:3); and again: "You must also make yourself a prince over us" (16:13). In other words, the opponents challenge the idea that Moses has received a special mission from God, they deny that he was sent by God. As punishment for this revolt, Korah, Dathan and Abiram along with their families, are going to be swallowed up by the earth. This catastrophe will be the sign that Moses has indeed been sent by God and that he has never acted "on his own", i.e., by claiming for himself an authority which he did not have.

Let us now place in parallel John 8:28b and John 12:49a, 50b, which form a doublet, underlining the borrowings from Num 16:28:

8:28b	12:49a, 50b
τότε γνώσεσθε ὅτι...	ὅτι ἐγὼ
ἀπ' ἐμαυτοῦ ποιῶ οὐδὲν	ἐξ ἐμαυτοῦ οὐκ ἐλάλησα
ἀλλὰ	ἀλλ' ὁ πέμψας με πατήρ...
καθὼς ἐδίδαξέν με ὁ πατὴρ	καθὼς εἴρηκέν μοι ὁ πατὴρ
ταῦτα λαλῶ.	οὕτως λαλῶ
καὶ ὁ πέμψας με...	

8:28b	12:49a, 50b
... then *you will know that...*	for I
I do nothing on my own	I have *not* spoken *on my own*
but	but the Father *who sent me...*
as the Father has taught me,	as the Father said to me,
these things I speak.	so I speak.
And he *who sent me...*	

The most characteristic borrowing, common to the two parallel texts, is the formula "not on my own". It is used in a context simiular to that of Num 16:28, more clearly in John 8:28 than in 12:49-50. Here again, the borrowing from the Numbers text is certain. Jesus speaks therefore in the same way as Moses.

b) Exod 4:12

ועתה לך ואנכי אהיה עם פיך והוריתיך אשר תדבר

καὶ νῦν πορεύου καὶ ἐγὼ ἀνοίξω τὸ στόμα σου καὶ συμβιβάσω σε ὃ μέλλεις λαλῆσαι

"And now, go! And I will open your mouth to *teach you what you will speak*" (LXX).

The context is the call of Moses. In place of "I will be with your mouth" (TM), the Septuagint translates by "I will open your mouth". The rest is translated literally, but with the verb λαλεῖν to translate תדבר as in Deut 18:18-19.

We find an echo of this text at the end of John 8:28, when Jesus says: "… but *I speak* thus as the Father *taught me*". In this form, the theme is not found elsewhere in the Bible.

c) Exod 3:12

כי אהיה עמך וזה לך האות כי אנכי שלחתיך

ἔσομαι μετὰ σοῦ καὶ τοῦτό σοι τὸ σημεῖον ὅτι ἐγώ σε ἐξαποστέλλω

"*For I will be with you*, and that (will be) for you the sign that *I am sending you*…".

The Septuagint translates the Hebrew text faithfully. The context is still that of the call of Moses: God entrusts him with a very special mission: to free his brothers from Egyptian bondage by going to find Pharaoh to demand of him that he let the Hebrews go (Exod 3:7-10). But Moses is afraid of this interview with Pharaoh (3:11) and God then gives him the assurance that he will be with him to help him in his mission (3:12).

Although the theme is frequent in the prophetic literature, we could think, given the preceding allusions, that John 8:29b echoes this text when Jesus says: "… and he *who has sent me is with me*".

d) To be complete, let us note that the expression "to do what is pleasing" to God has an Old Testament resonance. It is best preserved in 1 John 3:22: "We do what is pleasing to him". It occurs often in the calls for obedience which Moses makes to the Hebrews. The most interesting passage is Exod 15:26: "If you will diligently hearken to the voice of the Lord your God, and do that which is right in his eyes, and give heed to his commandments…" (cf. Deut 6:18; 12:25; 13:19; 21:9; etc.).

Thus John 8:28-29 consists of a series of OT textual reminiscences which are all related to Moses. The parallel between Jesus and Moses is undeniable.

3. *John 14:10 and 7:16b-17*

These two texts continue the characteristic formula "not of my self" in contexts which recall Num 16:28.

a) John 14:10

> The words that I say to you I do *not* speak *on my own authority*; but the Father who dwells in me *does his works*.

The context is the same as in John 8:28 and 12:49-50. We could then think that the formula "not of my self" takes up the phrase from Num 16:28. This is confirmed by the theme "do the works", even if there is a shift from Moses as the agent in Numbers to God in John. We will see further on that John 14 evokes the Exodus theme, and this makes the connection between John 14:10 and Num 16:28 all the more natural.

b) John 7:16b-17

> My teaching is not mine, but *his who sent me*; if any man's will is to do his will, he shall know whether the teaching is from God or whether I am speaking *on my own authority*.

The connection with Num 16:28 is here again rather clear. We could also refer to a rabbinic text, attested in Sifre Deut 5: "Moses said: It is not on my own that I speak to you, but I speak to you from the mouth of God".

4. *John 17:8*

> For I have given them *the words which thou gavest me*, and they have received them... and they have believed that thou didst send me.

This text must be interpreted in function of the developments which we have explained on John 12:48-50. The first part of this verse 8 calls up the text of Deut 18:18: "*I will give* (cf. LXX) my words in his mouth and he will say to them...". The theme of the disciples who have "received" the words must correspond, as in 12:48, to that of "hearing" the words which we read in Deut 18:19. Finally, the ending of the verse could be an allusion to Num 16:28: "By this you will know that God has sent me..." since the text is also in the background of John 12:49a.

But we can pursue the analysis of the passage even further. In 17:6, Jesus declares: "I have manifested thy name to the men", a theme which will be taken up as an inclusion in v. 26: "I made known to them thy name". If v. 8 contains a discreet allusion to the theme of the Prophet like Moses, we could think that vv. 6 and 26 refer implicitly to the story of the Sinai theophany, the episode of the burning bush. In Exod 3:13-14, Moses objects to God: "If I come to the people of Israel and say to them, 'The God of your fathers has sent me to you', they will ask me, 'What is his name (τί ὄνομα αὐτῷ)?'". Then God reveals his name to Moses: "I am who I am", or more clearly in Greek: "I am He Who Is" (ἐγώ εἰμι ὁ ὤν), or "I am the Being". And he adds: "You will say to them: 'I am' has sent me to you... This is my name forever". Moses has thus received revelation of the name of God: 'I am', or 'the Being', and he has handed it on to the children of Israel. In the same way Jesus, the Prophet like Moses: he has made known to men the Name of God.

5. *The Crucifixion: John 19: 17-18*

> ... he went out to the place called the place of a skull, which is called in Hebrew Golgotha. There they crucified him, and with him two others, one on either side, and Jesus between them.

A patristic tradition, already known to the author of the Epistle of Barnabas (12:9), around 130, but developed especially by the apologist Justin, around 150 (Dial 49:8; 90:4; 131:4-5), compares Jesus on the cross to Moses, who, helped by Aaron and Hur, keeps his arms outstretched to enable the Hebrews to overcome the Amalekites (Exod 17:8-13). In this typological interpretation of the Exodus story, the Amalekites symbolize all the powers of evil, demons and fallen angels, which Christ has overcome by dying, his arms outstretched on the cross. Is this parallelism between Jesus and Moses already attested in the Fourth Gospel? This is what we will examine now.

But before we analyze the crucifixion story, we must return to the saying of Jesus presented in John 12:31-32:

> Now is the judgment of this world, now shall the ruler of this world be cast down; and I, when I am lifted up from the earth, will draw all people to myself.

At v. 31, contrary to all the critical editions, we have adopted the reading "shall be cast down" (βληθήσεται κάτω) in place of "shall be cast out" (ἐκβληθήσεται ἔξω), with the following witnesses: Θ 1093 Epiphanius Chrysostom b e ff² r and Syrˢ (the simple verb, without the prefix, is also attested in P⁶⁶ D a c). This reading is recommended by the parallels in Luke 10:18 and Rev 12:9. The rise and evolution of the variants can be explained in this way. The κάτω of the original text would have fallen out through haplography before the κἀγώ which follows it. To make the text comprehensible, a scribe would have added the adverb ἔξω (cf. the reading of P⁶⁶ D a c) under the influence of texts like Luke 13:28; 14:35; John 15:6; Matt 13:48; 21:39; cf. 8:12. They would then have added the prefix to the verb to arrive at a rather common formula in the gospels (Matt 21:39; Mark 12:8; Luke 13:28; 20:15; John 6:37; 9:34-35).

This text sets up an opposition between Satan, the Prince of this world, and Jesus. While the first is "cast down", the second is "lifted up from the earth". As often in the Fourth Gospel, this is a phrase with a double meaning which refers both to the lifting up on the cross and elevation to the right hand of God. According to a notion current in NT times, Satan was thought to rule the world (cf. 1 John 5:19), whence all the evil found there. If he is "cast down", it is the sign that his domination of the world is coming to an end (cf. Luke 10:18; Rev 12:9). This event coincides with the lifting up of Christ on the cross, which will draw all people to him. To the reign of Satan must succeed the reign of Christ. The cross marks this reversal of the situation; it is then by dying on the cross that Christ has overcome Satan. Moreover, texts like John 13:27, 30 and 14:30-31 show that this fight of Jesus against Satan remains in the background of the Johannine Passion accounts[22]. We pick up here again the typological interpretation of the story in Exod 17:8-13; as Moses, arms outstretched, caused the defeat of the Amalekites, so too Christ, arms outstretched on the cross, caused the defeat of the forces of evil.

Let us reread now the story of the crucifixion. The three Synoptics indicate that Jesus was crucified between two thieves (Matt 27:38; Mark 15:27; Luke 23:33). All three use almost the same formula "one at (his) right and one at (his) left". But the Johannine text is very different. First, it suppresses the indication that the two other condemned men were thieves, and to indicate the respective position of the crucified, it has this formula: "... one on either side, and Jesus between them". The commentators ordinarily recognize that the Greek formula ἐντεῦθεν καὶ ἐντεῦθεν is a Semitism which corresponds to the Hebrew מזה אחד ומזה אחד; this is also how Delitzsch translates John's text into Hebrew[23]. Now let us return to the story of the Hebrews' fight against the Amalekites. To support Moses, the

22. See also Luke 4:13; 22:3; 22:53.
23. Franz Delitzsch, *Die vier Evangelien ins Hebräische übersetzt* (Traductions hébraïques des Évangiles rassemblées par Jean Carmignac, 4), Turnhout, Brepols, 1984, p. 201.

two men who accompanied him stood "one on either side". The Hebrew text corresponds exactly to what Delitzsch gives for John 19:18, and the Septuagint translates literally ἐντεῦθεν εἷς καὶ ἐντεῦθεν εἷς. Why does John differ here from the synoptic tradition? Why does he insist on the fact that Jesus was "in the middle"? Why above all does he here use a Semitic formula in a passage which contains no other? Probably because, for a reader used to the Jesus/Moses parallel, which runs throughout the gospel, he wants to insinuate that Jesus, arms outstretched on the cross, has overcome Satan just as Moses, his arms outstretched and supported by Hur and Aaron, overcame the Amalekites.

Let us add two details which connect the two events. In the Exodus account, Moses climbs to the top of a hill; in the same way, Jesus will be crucified at the place of the skull, which was a little rise of ground. In Aramaic, the same word means "head" and "top" or "summit". Moreover, Jesus, like Moses, remained with his arms extended until sunset (Exod 17:12; cf. John 19:31ff).

6. *The Exodus of Jesus (13:1; 14:1ff)*

a) The Passover of Jesus (13:1)

> Now before the feast of *the Passover*, when Jesus knew that his hour had come *to depart* [pass] out of this world to the Father...

According to Johannine chronology, differing in this from the Synoptics, Jesus dies on the very day of Passover, at the hour when the lambs were slaughtered in the Temple (cf. John 18:28). It is therefore Passover day when Jesus passes from this world to the Father. We will not here try to analyse the much disputed word Passover (*Pesach*). We will simply use the interpretation of it given by Philo of Alexandria: "For he (Moses) says: You must sacrifice the Passover in haste; the word is translated by 'passage' (διάβασις)" (*De Migr. Abrah.*, 25). Elsewhere, he interprets Passover as the "passage" (διάβασις) of the Red Sea by the Hebrews, that is, the passing from Egypt, symbol of the passions, to the Promised Land, symbol of freedom (*Leg. Alleg.*, iii, 94, 154). But the most interesting text for us is this: "This is the Passover of the soul, to use the exact word, this passage (διάβασις) from all that is passion and sentient to what is... intelligible and divine" (*Cong. erud. gratia*, 106)[24]. Philo

24. Transl. Monique Alexandre, *Les œuvres de Philon d'Alexandrie*, vol. 16 (Paris: Cerf, 1967).

here is certainly thinking of death: the moment when the immortal soul leaves the body, bound to the world of the senses, to find again the intelligible, divine world.

The analogy between John 13:1 and this passage from Philo is obvious. On Passover day, Jesus, by dying, is going "to pass" (ἵνα μεταβῇ) from this evil world (1 John 5:19) to the Father. Following Philo, the evangelist must make a connection between the "Passover" and the "passing" of Jesus from this world to the Father. Philonic influence on this text of John is all the more likely in that its way of speaking about death is not Semitic, but more or less Platonizing. In the Jewish tradition, at death the human goes down to sheol, a place of darkness where he lives as a shadow totally deprived of life. It is true that the Pharisaic current following the prophet Daniel (12:1-2), had admitted the belief in a future resurrection, but such a belief did not suppress the reality of sheol: it is there that the dead must await the day of resurrection. Even in the case of Christ, to say that Jesus is going "to pass from this world to the Father" does not agree with Semitic thought. This way of speaking does correspond on the contrary to a more or less Platonizing way of thinking. At death, the soul of the person leaves the body to set off for the world of the Ideas, for the world of the divine.

The theme of Passover, and thus of the Exodus, is present in this way in the background of the Johannine Passion narratives.

> b) In my Father's house are many rooms; if it were not so, would I have told you that *I go to prepare a place for you*? And when I go and *prepare a place for you*, I will come again and will take you to myself, that where I am you may be also. And you know *the way* where I am going (14:2-4).

The first italicized text is a quasi-quotation of Deut 1:33, read in the Targum[25] rather than in the TM or the Septuagint:

TM	ההלך לפניכם בדרך לתור לכם מקום
Targ.	דדבר קדמיכן בארחא למתקנה לכן אתר
TM	who went before you in the way to seek you out a place
Targ.	*who went* before you in the way *to prepare a place for you*

Jesus does not walk ahead of his disciples, but he leaves before they do to prepare a place for them. The idea is the same. Moreover,

---

25. We quote here Targum Neofiti as it was published by A. Diez Macho, *Neophyti 1. Targum Palestinense. Ms de la Biblioteca Vaticana. Tomo V: Deuteronomio* (Textos y Estudios 11), 1978. The Targum of Pseudo-Jonathan offers an analogous text; the verb which interests us is the same, but in a different form.

the text of Deut 1:33 explains that God (or his Word, in the Targum) will walk ahead of the Hebrews to point out for them *the route/way* where they should walk. In the gospel of John, Jesus says to the disciples that they know the way on which he sets forth (v. 4). But Thomas points out that, not knowing where he is going, they do not know the way (v. 5). Jesus answers that he himself is the way (v. 6). This insistence on the idea of knowing the way brings us back to the text of Deut 1:33.

Let us complete the parallelism between the two texts by making the following remarks. In Deut 1:29, Moses says to the Hebrews: "Do not be in dread or afraid of them"; in John 14:1a, Jesus begins his discourse by saying to the disciples: "Let not your hearts be troubled", that is, "Do not be afraid" (cf. 14:27). In Deut 1:31, Moses reproaches the Hebrews: "You did not believe the Lord your God..."; in John 14:1b, Jesus says to his disciples: "You believe in God, believe also in me...".

Given all these literary associations, it is hard not to see an influence of Deut 1:29-33 on the redaction of John 14:1ff.

7. *Moses or Jesus (9:26ff)*

In the light of all these texts which present Jesus as the prophet like Moses announced in Deut 18:18, the discussion between the man born blind who has just been cured by Jesus and the Jewish authorities, in John 9:26ff, gains a sharper focus. The Jews ask the formerly blind man a second time in what way Jesus opened his eyes (v. 26). He answers them then, with some impatience and much humor: "I have told you already, and you would not listen. Why do you want to hear it again? Do you too want to become his disciples?" (v. 27). The Jews then make their profession of faith in Moses: "They reviled him, saying, 'You are his disciple, but we are disciples of Moses. We know that God has spoken to Moses, but as for this man, we do not know where he comes from'". The problem is well posed: one must now choose between Moses and Jesus, between Moses and the prophet like him, announced in Deut 18:18. The mission of Jesus by God is authenticated by the miraculous cure which he has just worked (vv. 30-32). Rather than recognize it, the Jews are driven to deny the miracle, against all probability. They chose to remain faithful to the first Moses, despite the promise made by God in Deut 18:18 and the miracle which authenticates the mission of Jesus. But as for the blind man who has just been healed, he has chosen the new Moses.

C. *The Call of Nathanael*

In the story of Nathanael's call (1:45-49), Jesus is presented, not only as the prophet like Moses announced by Deut 18:18, but also as the king of Israel, successor of the patriarch Joseph, in the perspective of Samaritan traditions. Before showing this, we should first clarify the structure of the larger ensemble (1:19-51) of which this brief narrative is a part.

1. *The Thematic Unity of the Ensemble 1:19-51*

This ensemble is scanned by a succession of days which are carefully noted: "the next day" (vv. 29, 35, 43), then "on the third day" (2:1). Since, in spite of the absence of any chronological notice, the episode of the call of Peter (vv. 41-42) certainly occurs one day after the events recorded in 1:35-39, according to v. 39, many authors conclude that the total unit formed by 1:19–2:11 could be divided into seven days. We do not insist on this point which has little importance for our concern. We will rather note that, beyond this artificial chronological division, we can distinguish two parts in the section formed by vv. 19 to 51. The first part concerns the witness borne by John the Baptist to Jesus, in vv. 19-34. This witness is announced from the start of v. 19: "This is the testimony of John..."; it is described in vv. 32-34: "And John bore witness saying... And I have seen and have borne witness...". The second part is formed by the story of the call of Jesus' first disciples: Andrew and one of his companions (vv. 35-40), Simon Peter (vv. 41-42), Philip (vv. 43-44) and Nathanael (vv. 45-51).

This second part contains an internal unity which is worth noting. At vv. 35-39, two disciples of the Baptist undertake to follow Jesus. The evangelist gives us the name of the first one, Andrew (v. 40), but not of the second. A number of commentators have tried to lessen this silence by advancing the name of John, the son of Zebedee, the presumed author of the gospel. We think that the second disciple, who is not named in vv. 35-40, is Philip who will reappear in vv. 43ff. Here are the reasons in favor of this hypothesis. In vv. 35-40, two disciples of Jesus appear who are closely associated with each other. They are first alone with John the Baptist, then they follow Jesus, the two of them together. They already form a "pair". Now, in the gospel tradition, Andrew and John are never associated in any special way. If John is ever associated with another disciple, that other disciple is his brother James[26], never Andrew. On the other hand, in John's gospel, Andrew is always in Philip's company: they form a pair of inseparable friends (John 6:7-8; 12:20-22). It is therefore normal to suppose that, in 1:35-39, the companion of Andrew must already be Philip.

This hypothesis is strengthened by what the evangelist himself tells us. In 1:7, he affirms of John the Baptist: "He came for testimony, to bear witness to the light, that all might believe through him". The faith of *all people* must therefore depend on the witness of the Baptist. But if Philip is not one of the two disciples mentioned in 1:35-39, his faith in Jesus does not depend on the Baptist's witness, nor does that of Nathanael. On the other hand, if Philip was the disciple companion of Andrew spoken of in vv. 35-39, everything becomes clear. His faith and Andrew's depend on the Baptist's witness (vv. 35-39). Thanks to them, the faith of Simon Peter (vv. 40-42), then that of Nathanael (vv. 45-49), are connected to the Baptist's witness. Thanks to them again, the faith of the Greeks (12:20-22) depends on the Baptist's witness. Simon and Nathanael represent the Jewish world, the Greeks the pagan or Gentile world. It is then the whole world that, by the intermediary of Andrew and Philip, believe in Jesus thanks to the Baptist's witness, as the evangelist announced in 1:7.

Against this hypothesis, one could object that, in 1:43, Jesus seems to "meet" Philip for the first time. But in 5:14 and 9:35, we see that Jesus "meets" again people that he had left a short time before. And this presentation of the call of Philip, in v. 43, corresponds to a parallelism which the evangelist wants to set up, as we will see later, between the calls of Andrew and of Simon Peter on the one hand (vv. 35-42), of Philip and Nathanael on the other (vv. 43-51).

In this way, one sees better how the whole second part of the ensemble formed by vv. 19-51 depends on the first part. The first

---

26. Mark 1:19, 29; 3:17; 5:37; 9:2; 10:35, 41; 13:3; 14:33.

part concerns the Baptist's witness (vv. 19-34); the second part shows how the faith of the first four disciples depends on the witness of the Baptist (vv. 35-51). The link between the two parts is underlined by the repetition of the phrase by which John refers to Jesus: "This is the lamb of God" (vv. 29 and 35), as also by Nathanael's confession of faith: "You are the king of Israel" (v. 49), which corresponds to the mission which John received from God: to show the Messiah to Israel (v. 31). It was important, we will see later, to underline the thematic unity of the literary whole formed by vv. 19 to 51.

2. *"Him of whom Moses wrote in the Law" (v. 45)*

In v. 45, Philip declares to Nathanael: "We have found him of whom Moses in the law and also the prophets wrote...". The general reference to the Old Testament is obvious. But how should we understand it? How in particular should we interpret the formula "him of whom Moses wrote in the law"? With R.E. Brown, we think that this formula sends the reader to a quite precise text: the announcement of a sending by God of a prophet like Moses, according to Deut 18:18. Here are the reasons.

a) According to Bultmann, followed by Schnackenburg and Haenchen, the expression "the Law and the Prophets" corresponds to a stereotyped formula, frequent in the New Testament[27], and which refers to the whole of biblical revelation. Since the evangelist here speaks of the law and of the prophets, we need not look behind this formula for a reference to a definite text, but simply to a reference to the whole revelation of the Old Testament.

But in John 1:45, we do not have the stereotyped expression of which Bultmann speaks. Elsewhere in the New Testament, such an expression *always* implies that the nouns "Law" and "prophets" have the same function in the sentence, as in Matt 5:17: "Think not that I have come to abolish the law and the prophets", and in Rom 3:21 where Paul says of the righteousness of God that "the law and the prophets bear witness to it". In Greek, the two words are always in the same case and joined by a coordinating conjunction. The same is not the case in John 1:45 where we read "Him of whom Moses wrote in the law, and the prophets". The noun "the pro-

27. Matt 5:17; 7:12; 11:13; 22:40; Luke 16:16; 24:44; Acts 28:23; Rom 3:21.

phets" is the subject of the verb "wrote" and stands therefore in
parallel with "Moses", not with "the Law". But the pair "Moses...
the prophets" is not found elsewhere except in the Lucan writings[28]
and so we should no longer speak of a stereotyped formula which
occurs frequently in the New Testament. Indeed, it is found nowhere
else in the gospel of John. On the other hand, in John 5:46, we find
a text which clarifies this one: "If you believed *Moses*, you would
believe me, for *he wrote of me*". Here it is not a matter of the
prophets, but only of Moses, a fact which encourages us to dissociate in John 1:45 too Moses' witness from that of the prophets. We
are sent back to a text of the Pentateuch (Moses) announcing the
arrival of an eschatological figure.

   b) A number of texts could then be considered. First of all Deut
18:18 concerning the sending of a prophet like Moses. But also Gen
49:10: "The scepter shall not depart from Judah, nor the ruler's
staff from between his feet, until he comes to whom it belongs; and
to him shall be the obedience of the peoples". We could also think
of Balaam's oracle recorded in Num 24:17: "A star shall come forth
out of Jacob and a scepter shall rise out of Israel". These last two
texts announce the coming of *a king* belonging to the tribe of Judah
whereas the first speaks of the coming of a *prophet*. Lagrange thinks
that the Johannine text refers in an imprecise manner to this group
of texts.

   But we think that the proposition "Him of whom Moses wrote in
the law" refers very precisely to Deut 18:18, for the following
reasons.

   ba) The scene described in 1:45-49 supposes as background the
theme of Jesus prophet. Indeed, in view of Nathanael's reticence
"Can anything good come out of Nazareth?", Philip says to him:
"Come and see". Seeing Nathanael coming to him, Jesus declares:
"Behold, an Israelite indeed, in whom is no guile". Surprised,
Nathanael asks Jesus: "How do you know me?". And Jesus says to
him: "Before Philip called you, when you were under the fig tree, I
called you". Convinced, Nathanael then makes his profession of
faith: "Rabbi, you are the Son of God! You are the king of Israel!".
The mysterious meaning of Jesus' second statement to Nathanael (v.
48b) has been endlessly discussed. The precise fact to which Jesus

---

28. Luke 16:29, 31; 24:27; Acts 26:22.

alludes is of little importance to us. Let us simply retain the general sense of the dialogue: Jesus showed Nathanael that he was aware of an event of his life that he alone knew about. He thereby proved to him that he possessed supernatural knowledge, and this is what convinces Nathanael that Jesus is indeed "Him of whom Moses wrote in the law".

Now such supernatural knowledge is the characteristic of the prophet. In 2 Sam 12: 1-7, Nathan shows that he is a prophet because he reveals to king David that he is aware of an event which only David and Joab could have known about: the scheme which led to the death of Uriah the Hittite. But the parallel in John 4: 16-19 is even more convincing. Jesus reveals to the Samaritan woman that he is aware of her scandalous conduct: "You have had five husbands, and he whom you now have is not your husband" (4: 18). And the woman draws the conclusion: "Sir, I perceive that you are a prophet…" (v. 19). Similarly, a sinful woman washes Jesus' feet with her tears; scandalized, the Pharisee who had invited him says: "If this man were a prophet[29], he would have known who and what sort of woman this is who is touching him, for she is a sinner" (Luke 7: 39). Similarly in the present episode: the supernatural knowledge which Jesus has of an event which Nathanael should be the only one to know shows that he is a prophet. This leads us to think that the statement of Philip to Nathanael "Him of whom Moses wrote in the law" implies a prophetic incidence. It cannot refer then to anything other than Deut 18: 18.

bb) This is confirmed by the fact that this text of Deut 18: 18 holds a predominant place in John's gospel, as we have noted in the preceding sections. But a decisive text is 5: 46-47; we have quoted its first part above: "If you believed Moses, you would believe me, for *he wrote of me.* But if you do not believe his writings, how will you believe *my words?*". Jesus speaks here as a prophet who is imparting God's words to us. When he says that Moses has written of him, he is certainly alluding to Deut 18: 18 because, as we have noted earlier, Gen 49: 10 and Num 24: 17 are royal not prophetic oracles. We

---

29. The Vaticanus, supported by some minuscules, has the definite article: "the Prophet". This reading, dropped by the latest edition of Nestle-Aland, would go well in the direction of our developments.

could therefore think that, in 1:45 as well, the evangelist is only referring to Deut 18:18[30].

bc) In the Johannine narrative, we have in sequence the call of Simon Peter by the intermediary Andrew (vv. 40-42), then, almost immediately thereafter, the call of Nathanael by Philip as intermediary (vv. 45-49). These two scenes are structured according to a strict parellelism:

1:41-42	1:45-47
He first found Simon and said to him *"We have found the Messiah...*:	Philip found Nathanael and said to him: *"The one about whom Moses has written in the Law... we have found him..."*.
He brought him to Jesus. Having looked at him, Jesus said: You are Simon, son of John, you shall be called Cephas...".	Philip said to him: "Come and see". Jesus saw Nathanael and said of him: "Behold, a true Israelite...".

The two underlined formulas correspond then to one another. They can be seen in relation to those parallel confessions of faith of which we spoke in the first section:

7:40   This is truly the Prophet
7:41   This is the Christ

6:14   This is indeed the Prophet who is to come into the world
11:27 You are the Christ, the Son of God, he who is coming into the world.

We can conclude that, in 1:45, the phrase "He of whom Moses has written in the Law" refers to the text of Deut 18:18 announcing the coming of the Prophet like Moses, which makes parallel the titles "the Christ" and "the Prophet" as in 7:40-41 (cf. 6:14 and 11:27).

bd) In 7:52, high priests and Pharisees object to Nicodemus who wants to defend Jesus: "Are you from Galilee too? Search (the Scriptures) and you will see that the Prophet[31] does not come from Galilee". We find in 1:45-46 the same problematic. To Philip who says to him: "Him of whom Moses wrote in the Law... we have

---

30. In Nestle-Aland's manual critical edition of the Greek NT, the references to John 1:45 and to Deut 18:15 (parallel to 18:18) are placed in the margin of the volume facing John 5:46-47.

31. We have established above that we should read here "the Prophet", and not "a prophet".

found him, it is Jesus, the son of Joseph of Nazareth", Nathanael objects: "Can anything good come out of Nazareth?". The objection is based on the fact that Nazareth is found in Galilee. We are therefore invited to conclude that the formula of 1:45 "Him of whom Moses wrote in the Law" implies the title "the Prophet" expressed in 7:52. The text of 1:45 alludes therefore to Deut 18:18.

be) We said above that the section concerning the witness of John the Baptist (1:19-34) was closely linked to the section concerning the call of the first apostles (1:35-51). We note then that an antithetical parallel exists between John the Baptist and Jesus: the one is what the other is not. Note the solemnity with which the denials of the Baptist are presented: "And he confessed, he did not deny it, he confessed: 'I am not *the Christ*'. And they asked him: [what then are you, Elijah? And he said: I am not he.] Are you *the Prophet*? And he answered: No". In these denials of the Baptist, we find the parallelism between the titles "the Christ" and "the Prophet" which we have already noted in 7:40-41 and in 6:14; 11:27. To these solemn denials are opposed the two parallel confessions of faith made by Andrew and Simon Peter: "We have found the Messiah" (which means the Christ) (1:41), and by Philip to Nathanael: "Him of whom Moses has written in the Law... we have found him" (1:45). The one of whom Moses has written in the Law could be no other than the Prophet announced by God in Deut 18:18. Let us put the complete texts in parallel:

1:20-21	1:41, 45
He confessed it, he did not deny it. He confessed,	
"I am not the Christ"	"We have found the Messiah, which means Christ".
And they asked him: ["Are you Elijah?". And he replied: "I am not he".]	
"Are you the Prophet?"	"We have found him of whom Moses in the law and also the prophets wrote...".
He said: "No".	

b) Let us add a final argument. In this account, Philip presents Jesus to Nathanael by saying to him: "The one of whom Moses has written in the law... we have found him". Then Nathanael makes a profession of faith by saying to Jesus: "You are The Son of God, the king of Israel" (1:49). We will see further on that, in this text, the expression "Son of God" does not have a transcendent sense but denotes a royal prerogative. To Philip's profession of faith "The one of whom Moses has written of in the law" corresponds then the profession of Nathanael's "You are the king of Israel". If you admit that Philip's confession of faith implies the text of Deut 18:18 concerning the sending of a prophet like Moses, you obtain a close link between the titles "the Prophet" and "King of Israel", as in 6:14-15, at the conclusion of the story of the multiplication of the loaves: the crowds acclaim Jesus as "the Prophet who comes into the world" (v. 14), then they want to lay hold of him to make him king (v. 15).

For all these reasons, it seems certain to us that the formula used by Philip in 1:45 "The one of whom Moses has written in the Law" refers in a quite precise way to the text of Deut 18:18 and implies for Jesus the title "the Prophet" which the Baptist had refused for himself in 1:21.

3. *Recourse to Samaritan Traditions*

In v. 45 of the present narrative, Jesus is implicitly recognized by Philip as "the Prophet" announced by Moses in Deut 18:18. At the same time, he is designated as "the son of Joseph". Moreover, in v. 49, Nathanael is going to proclaim him "king of Israel". Moses, Joseph, prophet, king... This convergence of proper names and titles invites us to investigate the Samaritan traditions as they appeared in the treatise of a theologian of the 4th century A.D. which has reached us under the name of *Memar Marqah*, Words of Marqah[32].

For the Samaritans, two people stand out in their importance from all those who are mentioned in the Pentateuch: the patriarch Joseph and the prophet Moses[33]. The exceptional importance given to Moses[34] is explained by the fact that, of all the books of the Old Testament, the Samaritans recognized as inspired Scripture only the

---

32. Text edited by J. MacDonald, *Memar Marqah. The Teaching of Marqah. Edited and Translated.* 2 vol. (BZAW, 84), Berlin, 1963.

33. See the work of Meeks, *The Prophet-King*, pp. 220ff.

34. Cf. J. MacDonald, *The Theology of the Samaritans* (NT Library), London, 1964, pp. 147-222. This author has clearly set forth the exceptional importance of Moses in Samaritan theology. On the other hand, he did not stress sufficiently the importance of the patriarch Joseph.

Pentateuch, whose editing they dated back to Moses. As for the patriarch Joseph, father of Ephraim and of Manasseh, he was the ancestor starting from whom the northern tribes distinguished themselves from those of the south, and thus he was the ancestor of the Samaritans, descendants of the northern tribes. Now they commonly gave Joseph the title of king, basing this on the accounts of Genesis. In Gen 37, Joseph tells his family of a dream he had had: his brothers' sheaves bowed down before his sheaf and they asked him: "Would you then reign over us as king, or rule as master?" (37:8). Yes, Joseph will become king, but in Egypt. After having explained Pharaoh's dream about the seven fat cows and the seven lean cows, Joseph finds himself invested by him with full powers over Egypt: "It is you who will be master of my palace, and my people will obey your orders; only as regards the throne will I be greater than you... Behold, I have set you over all the land of Egypt... Then was he set over all the land of Egypt" (Gen 41:40-43). Forcing the texts a bit, the Samaritans based the kingship of Joseph on this. This is what Marqah admits when he writes: "Joseph came: he was rewarded with a kingdom after his enslavement" (*Memar Marqah*, 4:12).

Two people, then, dominate the whole history of Israel: Moses the prophet and Joseph the king. To honor them together, Marqah often places them side by side:

> The Taheb will come in peace to reign over the place which God has chosen for pious people. Joseph came, he was rewarded with a kingdom after his enslavement and those who oppressed him sought his favors... There is no one like *Joseph the king*, and no one like *Moses the prophet*. Both of them possessed an elevated position: Moses possessed prophecy and Joseph possessed the good mountain (i.e., Garizim). There is no one greater than these two (*Memar Marqah*, iv:12).

There is an analogous text in the Durran, a collection of liturgical texts incorporated in the Defter[35] and which were composed by Amram Darah, a contemporary of Marqah:

> And after his death, Joseph was glorified, his bones were carried back by the great Prophet (i.e., Moses) who had been called "god" by him who reigns. Two men in whom God was well pleased: *Joseph the king and Moses the Prophet* (*Durran* 22).

The last part of this text bids us take another look at vv. 45 and 49 of the Johannine account where we find placed together, we

35. A.E. Cowley, *The Samaritan Liturgy*, vol. 1, 1909.

recall, the names of *Moses* and of *Joseph* (v. 45), the title of *king*
given to Jesus (v. 49) and, implicitly, the theme of the *Prophet* like
Moses announced in Deut 18:18 (v. 45). This cannot be the effect of
chance. It is true that in v. 45, it is a matter of Joseph, the father of
Jesus, and not the patriarch. But does not this proper name cover
two persons, first the father of Jesus, but also in the background, the
patriarch of the same name? Let us pursue our analyses in order to
clarify this point.

4. *Jesus King, in Imitation of the Patriarch Joseph*

The answer to the question which we have just asked is given in
the episode which follows immediately the narrative of the call of
Nathanael, namely the miracle of the water changed into wine at the
wedding of Cana (2:1-11). In redacting this narrative, the evangelist
wants to establish a parallel between Jesus, who obtains wine for
those who have no more, and the patriarch Joseph who obtained
bread for the Egyptians who were deprived of it because of the great
drought which had just fallen upon Egypt (Gen 41). It suffices to
place the Johannine account in parallel with Gen 41:55 to realize
this:

Gen 41:55	John 2
And all the land of Egypt was hungry and the people cried out to Pharaoh for bread.	3. And, the wine beginning to run out, the mother of Jesus said to him: "They have no more wine".
	4. Jesus said to her: "What is there between you and me, woman? My hour has not yet come".
And Pharaoh said to all the Egyptians: "Go to Joseph; and what he tells you to do, do it".	5. The mother of Jesus said to the servants: "What he tells you to do, do it".

Not only do the two accounts offer a parallel scheme, in spite of the
addition offered by the Johannine text (v. 4), but v. 5 of John
contains an almost literal quotation of Gen 41:55c. The influence of
this latter text on the redaction of John 2:3-5 is certain. But, we
recall, according to Samaritan traditions, Joseph would have been
appointed by the Pharaoh king over Egypt precisely in view of
giving bread to the starving Egyptians. Likewise, in John's gospel,
Jesus is proclaimed "king of Israel" just before the episode of the
wedding at Cana. It is easy to see then the parallelism of the
situations. The Egyptians have no more bread; the guests at the

wedding in Cana have no more wine. According to Samaritan traditions, Joseph had just been installed as king by Pharaoh; in John's gospel, Jesus had just been recognized as king by Nathanael. To alleviate the lack of bread, Pharaoh sends the Egyptians to Joseph telling him: "All that he tells you to do, do it"; to alleviate the lack of wine, Mary sends the servants to Jesus, telling them: "All that he tells you to do, do it". By this quotation of Gen 41:55, the evangelist wishes to point out to us that the kingship of Jesus, proclaimed just before by Nathanael, is in the image of that of the patriarch Joseph. Under the influence of Samaritan traditions, the original theme of v. 45 is enriched by a new harmony: as "prophet" Jesus is like Moses, but as "king", he resembles the patriarch Joseph. Jesus therefore realizes in his person the expectation of the eschatological hope of the Samaritan people.

Let us add an important detail. The phrase of Mary to the servants "All that he tells you to do, do it" (2:5) refers we just said to Gen 41:55. But it has a double meaning. In effect, how could we not *also* think of the text of Deut 18:15, 18-19: the Prophet like Moses will tell men what God has commanded him, they must listen to him, obey him, and then do what he says. The sentence must then have a very general meaning, as in Luke 6:46: "Why do you call me 'Lord, Lord' and do not do what I tell you to do?" (cf. Matt 7:24, 26). Mary tells the servants to obey the orders given by Jesus to remedy the lack of wine, but beyond this immediate meaning, we must also understand that it is asked of all men to act in conformity with what the Prophet tells us from God's side. In 2:5 as in 1:45, the two themes are blended: Jesus, the Prophet like Moses, and Jesus the king of Israel, descendant and heir of the patriarch Joseph.

5. *Jesus, "son of Joseph" (1:45)*

If we grant the foregoing analyses, we are led to ask ourselves whether, in John 1:45, the expression "son of Joseph" did not have a double meaning. At first, Jesus would be designated as son of Joseph, the carpenter of Nazareth, but also as son of Joseph the patriarch to whom the Samaritans had given the title of king[36]. The expression "son of Joseph" would then have a value analogous to that of "son of David" in use in the Judean tradition. According to

---

36. Cf. already in this sense G.W. Buchanan, "The Samaritan Origin of the Gospel of John", p. 160.

this tradition, David was the king par excellence, founder of a dynasty which would never be extinguished (2 Sam 7:12-16): by the title of "son of David" the Judean tradition designated a descendant of David who would inherit his royal prerogatives[37]. Similarly, in the perspective of the Samaritan traditions, the title "son of Joseph" could have designated the descendant and heir of the royal privileges of the patriarch Joseph. Is it possible to recover the traces of such a set of titles in the Samaritan traditions?

It is true that, in Samaritan literature, the Taheb, a figure of eschatological times, is never called "son of Joseph". But the first witnesses of this literature go back only to the fourth century of our era, and from their silence we cannot conclude that the Samaritans did not know of the use of that title in New Testament times. It is therefore necessary to take up the problem again, by broadening the perspectives[38].

a) Let us start with the surest data: those of the rabbinic tradition. The eschatological expectations of two Messiahs is quite well attested, both at Qumran, and in the rabbinic tradition. At Qumran, they are not named; but in the rabbinic tradition, the one was called "son of David" and the other "son of Joseph" or else "son of Ephraim". We read for example in the Targum on Cant 4:2, an admittedly late text:

> Your two saviors who ought to deliver you, *the Messiah son of David and the Messiah son of Ephraim*, are like Moses and Aaron

משיח בר דוד ומשיח בר אפראים

An older text, and which presents itself as traditional, is given in the Babylonian Talmud:

> Our teachers have handed on to us: *The Messiah son of David*, who ought to be revealed soon, in our time, God will say to him: "Ask something of me and I will give it to you"... When therefore he saw that the *Messiah son of Joseph* was killed, he says in his presence: "Master of the world, I only ask you for life..."[39].

משיח בן דוד ... משיח בן יוסף

---

37. Cf. Matt 9:27; 12:23; 15:22; 20:30f; 21:15; and parallels.
38. Cf. M.-J. Lagrange, *Le messianisme chez les Juifs* (Études Bibliques), Paris, 1909, pp. 251-256. G.H. Dix, "The Messiah ben Joseph", *JTS* 27 (1926) 130-143. C.C. Torrey, "The Messiah Son of Ephraim", *JBL* 66 (1947) 253-277.
39. Baraitha *Sukka* 52a.

The two Messiahs ought then to have a different fate. The Messiah son of David alone is called to rule over the eschatological world, while the Messiah son of Joseph will be killed as he leads the great battle which must precede the advent of the new world.

But the oldest text, and for us the most interesting, has handed down to us a saying attributed to Rabbi Dosa, a rabbi of the Tannaitic period who probably lived, either at the end of the first century or in the middle of the second. This text deals with a controversy on the traditional interpretation of the oracle in Zech 12: 10: "They looked upon him whom they had pierced":

> There was a controversy between Rabbi Dosa and our teachers. The one said: "This refers to the Messiah Son of Joseph that he would be killed". And the other said: "This refers to the evil tendency which must be killed". For him who says "It refers to the Messiah Son of Joseph who would be killed", that agrees well with what is written: "And they looked upon him whom they had pierced, and they wept over him as a beloved"[40].

A rabbinical tradition, which goes back at least to the beginning of the second century, knew then of the existence of a Messiah who would be put to death, and that tragic event would be the realization of the oracle of Zech 12: 10: "they will look upon him whom they have pierced". We need to ask two questions in regard to this tradition: what is the provenance of this title "son of Joseph", and was it already known in the New Testament period?

b) The title "son of Joseph" could only have developed in the Samaritan tradition. By analogy with the title "son of David", it presupposes in effect a milieu which gave an exceptional importance to the patriarch Joseph and above all, one which considered him a king. But the person of Joseph does not hold a special place in Judean traditions and furthermore, he was never considered a king. Even the blessing of Moses concerning Joseph does not have a monarchical bearing: "First-born of the bull, to him be glory. His horns are the horns of the buffalo whose blows strike the peoples even to the ends of the earth. Such are the myriads of Ephraim, such are the myriads of Manassah" (Deut 33: 17). This oracle simply wants to affirm the victory of Joseph and of his descendants over their enemies, like the parallel blessing of Gen 49: 22ff upon which it depends. Contrast the oracle of Gen 49: 10 where it is prophesied:

40. Baraitha *Sukka* 52a.

"The scepter will not leave Juda, nor the staff of rule from between his feet". This oracle has a royal bearing, but it concerns Juda and not Joseph. On the other hand, we have seen above, the Samaritan tradition gave an exceptional place to the patriarch Joseph, whom it considered along with Moses as the principal figure in the early history of Israel, and it gave him the title of king.

It is in this direction that the Samaritan texts themselves point us. It is true that the Taheb, the eschatological figure of the Samaritan tradition, is never called "son of Joseph" in the texts which have come down to us[41]. But let us compare one of the other two passages of *Memar Marqah*:

> We are *the sons of Joseph* according to the decree; are we going to abandon *his kingdom*? That would not be just (4:6).

בני יוסף... מלכותה

In this first passage, we do indeed find the expression "sons of Joseph" and it is linked to the theme of kingship; but it is used in a collective sense. It is the Samaritan people as a whole who are called "son of Joseph" inasmuch as he is the heir of the kingdom which Joseph had possessed.

> The Taheb will come in peace, he will reign over the place God had chosen for this good people. Joseph came; he was rewarded with a kingdom after enslavement... (4:12).

The Taheb must rule and his kingdom will be the continuation of the one which Joseph received. So if the expression "sons of Joseph" could be applied, collectively, to the Samaritans as heirs of Joseph's kingdom, as is said in the previous text, how much more so can it apply to the Taheb, the future king of the Samaritans, and thus the heir par excellence of the kingship with which Joseph had been invested.

We conclude then by saying that the title "son of Joseph", to designate the heir of the eschatological kingdom, could only have arisen and developed in a Samaritan setting.

c) In the first half of the second century, Rabbi Dosa, as we have seen, echoes a rabbinical tradition according to which the Messiah son of Joseph would be put to death, fulfilling thus in his person the

41. On the Taheb in Samaritan traditions, see F. Dexinger, *Der Taheb. Ein "messianischer" Heilsbringer der Samaritaner* (Kairos: Religionswissenschaftliche Studien, 3), Salzburg, 1986.

oracle of Zech 12:10: "They looked upon him whom they had pierced". How old is this tradition? Certain clues permit us to think that one finds an echo of this in the fourth gospel.

It is remarkable in fact that it alone reports the following episode. Once Jesus had died on the cross, instead of breaking his legs, one of the Roman soldiers pierces his side with a spear. Thus is realized, according to the evangelist, the oracle of Zech 12:10: "They will see the one whom they have pierced" (John 19:37). This oracle is quoted two more times in the New Testament, in Matt 24:30 and Rev 1:7. But in these two passages it is coupled with a quotation from Dan 7:13 and concerns therefore the eschatological return of Christ. John 19:37 is then the only text of the New Testament which puts Zech 12:10 in relation with the death of the Christ, of the Messiah. Now the reader of the gospel, knowing the Johannine traditions, has certainly not forgotten that this Jesus who died on the cross is no other than the descendant and royal heir of the patriarch Joseph (1:49 and 2:5), and hence the "son of Joseph" (1:45).

The evangelist has moreover taken care to recall it. The cross on which Jesus dies carries the inscription "Jesus the Nazorean, king of the Jews" (John 19:19). Therefore it is as king that Jesus dies. This theme of the kingship of Christ had held a preponderant place in the Johannine account of Jesus' appearance before Pilate. With the Synoptics, John assumes that Jesus acknowledged his kingship before Pilate (18:33, 37), but alone of the four evangelists he terminates the scene with this dialogue between Pilate and the Jews: "Pilate said to them: 'Should I crucify your king?'. The high priests replied: 'We have no king but Caesar'. Then he released him to be crucified" (19:15-16). It is true that in 18:33 as in 19:19 Jesus is designated as "king of the Jews", but that is because John follows here the data of the synoptic tradition. On the other hand, at the time of the solemn entrance to Jerusalem, the day of palms, according to John 12:13 Jesus is acclaimed "king of Israel" whereas, according to Matt 21:9 and Mark 11:10, he is acclaimed a descendant of David. In the Johannine text, one returns to the confession of Nathanael in 1:49: "Rabbi, you are the son of God, you are the king of Israel". It is indeed the king of Israel, the son of Joseph, who dies on the cross.

A study of the structure of the gospel confirms the direct link
which exists between the beginning of Jesus' ministry and his death.
Jesus begins his public ministry by accomplishing the miracle of the
changing of water into wine, at the time of the wedding feast at
Cana in Galilee (2: 1-11). Mary, the mother of Jesus, is present at
this wedding feast and it is she who serves as "mediatrix" between
the wedding guests and Jesus. When Jesus dies on the cross, at the
end of his earthly life, Mary is again present and Jesus entrusts a
particular role to her by naming her "mother" of the beloved
disciple, who is the model of all those who would be his disciples by
believing in him (19: 25-27). In the two scenes, Jesus addresses his
mother by giving her the title "woman", and these are the only two
passages of the gospel where Mary appears. We are certainly in the
presence of a deliberate "inclusion" by the evangelist.

Now the episode of the wedding in Cana is immediately preceded
by the account of the calling of Nathanael (1: 45-51) to which it is
closely linked since, as we have seen, it is as "son of Joseph" (1: 45),
as "king of Israel" (1: 49), that Jesus performs a miracle at his
mother's request. Further, the account of Mary present at the foot
of the cross is immediately followed by the episode of the spear
thrust by the Roman soldier into Jesus' side, an episode whose
meaning is given by the quotation from Zech 12: 10 (John 19: 31-
37). These two episodes are also strictly linked since it is the disciple
whom Jesus loved, to whom Jesus entrusts his mother according to
19: 25-27, who can bear witness to the lance thrust by the Roman
soldier (19: 35). All these episodes are connected and we have
therefore a double inclusion in the form of a chiasm: to the account
of Jesus changing the water into wine at the wedding feast of Cana,
at the request of his mother (2: 1-11), corresponds the account of
Jesus on the cross who entrusts his mother to the beloved disciple
(19: 25-27). To the account of the calling of Nathanael, in which
Jesus is acknowledged as "son of Joseph" and as "king of Israel"
(1: 45-49) corresponds the episode of the lance thrust which is based
on the oracle of Zech 12: 10: "They will look upon him whom they
have pierced" (19: 37). It is then as "son of Joseph" that Jesus, dying
on the cross, fulfills the oracle of Zech 12: 10. This is, already
established, the tradition of which, later, Rabbi Dosa makes himself
an echo.

6. *The Gift of the Spirit*

In the call of Nathanael story (1:45-51), Jesus is, we have seen, presented as the one who comes to fulfill the eschatological hopes of the Samaritans, the descendants of the Northern Kingdom, the kingdom of Israel. He is, to be sure, the prophet like Moses promised by God in Deut 18:18. Formerly God spoke to Moses, putting in his mouth the words intended for his people. Today, God is going to speak through Jesus; it is by his mouth that he is going to address his people and to give them a new law. But Jesus is also "the son of Joseph". He is, in the strict sense, the son of Joseph, the carpenter from Nazareth; but this title contains another: he is the descendant and heir of the patriarch Joseph, invested with kingship by the Egyptian Pharaoh. As "son of Joseph" he can thus claim the title "king of Israel" which Nathanael bestows on him. He is simultaneously "the Prophet" and "the king of Israel".

If Jesus can claim these two titles, it is because he has just received the Spirit, as the Baptist testified (1:32-34). According to the whole biblical tradition it is the Spirit who inspires the prophets. This is true *a fortiori* for Moses, the greatest of all the prophets. When Moses complains to God that he finds it a burden too heavy to bear to lead the Hebrew people, God says to him:

> Gather for me seventy men of the elders of Israel, whom you know to be the elders of the people and officers over them; and bring them to the tent of meeting, and let them take their stand there with you. And I will come down and talk with you there; and I will take some of the spirit which is upon you and put it upon them; and they shall bear the burden of the people with you, that you may not bear it yourself alone (Num 11:16-17).

A little further on, the sacred author describes Moses' realization of this divine ordinance. The prophetic character of the scene is set out much more clearly:

> So Moses went out and told the people the words of the Lord; and he gathered seventy men of the elders of the people, and placed them round about the tent. Then the Lord came down in the cloud and spoke to him, and took some of the spirit that was upon him and put it upon the seventy elders; and when the spirit rested upon them, they prophesied. But they did so no more.
>
> Now two men remained in the camp, one named Eldad, and the other named Medad, and the spirit rested upon them; they were among those registered, but they had not gone out to the tent, and so they prophesied in the camp. And a young man ran and told Moses, "Eldad and Medad are prophesying in the camp". And Joshua the son of Nun, the minister of

Moses, one of his chosen men, said, "Are you jealous for my sake? Would that all the Lord's people were prophets, that the Lord would put his spirit upon them!" (Num 11:24-29).

If then Jesus can be the prophet like Moses announced in Deut 18:18, it is because he himself received the Spirit at his baptism. Similarly, Pharaoh wants to set the patriarch Joseph as king over the land of Egypt because he recognizes in him a more than ordinary wisdom which comes from this, that he possesses in himself the Spirit. After Joseph has interpreted Pharaoh's dream and recommended some measures intended to alleviate the lack of food during the years of drought, Pharaoh says to his officers: "Can we find such a man as this, in whom is the Spirit of God?" (Gen 41:38). And he sets him up as master of the palace over the whole land of Egypt.

Jesus possesses in himself the Spirit which he received at his baptism; he can thus by a singular privilege be at once the Prophet like Moses announced in Deut 18:18 and the King of Israel, descendant of the patriarch Joseph and heir of his kingdom.

7. *Return to Samaritan Traditions*

To establish the Samaritan origin of the gospel of John, we have depended in large part on the work of a Samaritan author of the fourth century: *Memar Marqah*. But would it not have been this relatively late author who would have used John's gospel?

a) The question poses itself all the more sharply since this Samaritan work offers other thematic contacts with Johannine literature. The most significant revolve around the idea of "truth". Let us cite some texts.

> There is no good life but the life of men *who know the truth and walk in it.* With uprightness, listen to the words of Moses so that your life may be always glorified in propserity (*MM* iv:5).

חכמו קשטה והלכו בה

Compare this with John 8:31-32: "If you remain in my word, you will truly be my disciples, and you will know the truth, and the truth will set you free". In 2 John 4 and 3 John 3:4, it is a matter of "walking in the truth".

> The Taheb will come in peace. He will possess the places of the perfect. He will manifest the truth. Lend an ear and listen and *hold yourself in the truth and purify your desires* (*MM* iv:12).

ואקים בקשטה וזרי עניניך

... the country of good things that the True One has promised to men who walk in obedience to him and who *keep themselves in the truth* (*MM* iii: 2).

Compare this with John 8:44: "You are from your father the devil and you want to do the desires of your father. He was a murderer from the beginning and he did not hold himself in the truth". Moreover in John 8:40, 45, Jesus presents himself as the one who says, and then reveals, the truth to men. Finally, God is called "the True One" in John 17:3, and 1 John 5:20.

You seek the covenant of Abraham, and *you do not do his works* (*MM* iii: 2).

ולא תעבד עובדין

The preceding texts bring us close to John 8:31-59. This one makes us think of John 8:39: "If you were children of Abraham, you would be doing the works of Abraham".

b) It is possible (but not certain) that, for these themes, Marqah depends on Johannine literature. On the other hand, we do not believe that he could depend on the fourth gospel for the double theme of Jesus the prophet like Moses and the royal heir of the patriarch Joseph. One would have to suppose that this Samaritan author had applied himself to an exegesis of John 1:45-49 of the subtle sort we have given, and that is very unlikely. Moreover, this theme of Jesus descendant and heir of the patriarch Joseph, the king of Israel, can only be conceived in a Samaritan perspective. We are therefore in the presence of specifically Samaritan Christological themes, put to work first by the author of the fourth gospel and then by Marqah.

Let us recall also that the gospel of John shows, moreover, a marked interest in Samaria, as witness the episode of the conversation of Jesus with the Samaritan woman (John 4:1-42) and also the mention of the baptism administred by John at Aenon near Salem, a place that should probably be localized in the very heart of Samaria[42].

---

42. Cf. M.-É. Boismard, "Aenon près de Salem (Jean, iii, 23)", *RB* 80 (1973) 218-229; reprinted in *Moïse ou Jésus*, pp. 145-158 (Appendix I).

D. *The First Three Signs*

In the source followed by the evangelist, the ministry of Jesus in Galilee began with three miracles that occurred in the following sequence:

2:1ff   Miracle of the water changed to wine at Cana of Galilee
2:12   Jesus goes down to Capharnaum with his mother, his brothers and his disciples
4:46bff   Cure of the son of the royal official, in Capharnaum
7:1ff   Jesus refuses to go up to Jerusalem and stays in Galilee
21:1ff   The miraculous catch of fish

This sequence had as its purpose to show that Jesus was the prophet like Moses announced by Deut 18:18. As Moses had to accomplish three "signs" in order to accredit among the Hebrews his mission from God (Exod 4:1ff), so Jesus, at the start of his ministry, had to accomplish three "signs" to be recognized as the envoy of God. This is what we must now demonstrate.

DA. *The First Two Miracles*

The hypothesis of a source, taken up by the evangelist, in which the miracle of the water changed into wine at the wedding of Cana (2:1ff) and the healing of the royal official's son at Capharnaum (4:46ff) follow immediately upon one another is not new. Proposed by Wellhausen[43] in 1908, it was taken up by Spitta[44] in 1910. But it is Bultmann who assured its success when he made of these two miracles the beginning of his *Semeia-Quelle* (signs-source). Since then it has been adopted by all those, and they are many, who have followed in the tracks of Bultmann. As F. Neirynck has written a propos of this sequence: "Here we easily recognize the reconstruction of the signs-source, which has become common coin in recent Johannine studies"[45].

---

43. Julius Wellhausen, *Das Evangelium Johannis*, Berlin, 1908, p. 14.
44. Fr. Spitta, *Das Johannes-Evangelium als Quelle der Geschichte Jesu*, Göttingen, 1910, pp. 63ff.
45. Frans Neirynck, *Jean et les Synoptiques. Examen critique de l'exégèse de M.-É. Boismard* (BETL 49), Leuven, 1979, p. 169. In this volume, written with four of his collaborators, Neirynck criticizes, among others, the positions which we are going to adopt in this chapter.

1. *The Classic Argument*

To prove the existence of a pre-Johannine document in which the miracles of the water changed into wine (2: 1ff) and the cure of the son of the royal official (4: 46ff) succeeded each other immediately, scholars depend above all upon John 2: 12: "He (Jesus) went down to Capharnaum, he and his mother, his brothers and disciples, and they stayed there a few days". This notice comes immediately after the episode of the wedding in Cana. From the following verse (2: 13), we learn that Jesus went up to Jerusalem for the Easter feast. Why mention this descent of Jesus to Capharnaum with all his entourage, and in such a solemn manner, if he did not exercise there any notable activity? This verse 12 demands a continuation that is absent from the present gospel. Now, in 4: 46b-54, Jesus goes to cure the son of a royal official who lives in Capharnaum. It is true that according to the gospel, in its present form, Jesus accomplishes this miracle at a distance, while he is, not in Capharnaum, but again at Cana of Galilee (v. 46a). Note however the two following points. On the one hand we read an analogous account in Matt 8: 5-13 and Luke 7: 1-10: Jesus cures the son of a centurion. Now, even if the cure is worked at a distance, as in the Johannine narration, Jesus is all the same in Capharnaum. Moreover, as Spitta has well noted, in John 4: 46a, we do not see why Jesus has returned to Cana of Galilee; this half verse poses an analogous problem to the one we have pointed out apropos of John 2: 12. All of these difficulties disappear if we admit that the evangelist depends on a source in which we had the following sequence: Jesus accomplishes the miracle of water changed into wine at the wedding of Cana (2: 1ff); then he goes down to Capharnaum with his whole entourage (2: 12) and there he cures the son of a royal official as in Matt and Luke (4: 46b-54)[46].

At the same time this hypothesis allows us better to comprehend why these first two miracles are like numbered items, and by means of similar formulas (2: 11 and 4: 54); but before developing this point it is necessary to pin down the meaning of these two formulas.

---

46. On this hypothesis, we must attribute to the Redactor, not only v. 46a, but also vv. 48-49 and other minor alterations.

2. The Formulas of 2:11 and of 4:54a

We shall only occupy ourselves for the moment with the first part of the formulas which serve as conclusion to the two miracles at Cana and at Capharnaum.

2:11 ταύτην ἐποίησεν ἀρχὴν τῶν σημείων ὁ Ἰησοῦς...
4:54 τοῦτο δὲ πάλιν δεύτερον σημεῖον ἐποίησεν ὁ Ἰησοῦς...

2:11 this did Jesus as a beginning of the signs...
4:54 this, again, did Jesus as the second sign...

a) It would be erroneous to translate 2:11 by "Jesus did this commencement of signs...". Such a translation would only be justified if one followed the text of the Koine, which adds the definite article before the noun ἀρχήν. As a matter of fact, the initial demonstrative in the feminine accusative ταύτην takes the place of a neuter accusative τοῦτο, direct object of the verb ἐποίησεν. It has been attracted to the gender of its attribute, ἀρχήν[47]. Without this grammatical particularity, one would have had: τοῦτο ἐποίησεν ἀρχὴν τῶν σημείων, a formula which approximates the one that is read in 4:54, whence the translation that we, along with almost all modern commentators, have adopted.

b) The majority of commentators and of translators understand 4:54 as we have: δεύτερον is an adjective that serves as epithet to the noun σημεῖον, and this last is attribute of the demonstraive τοῦτο. Haenchen has translated very well. "Dies hat Jesus wiederum als ein zweites Zeichen getan..."[48]. But F. Neirynck construes the phrase in a very different fashion[49]. For him, δεύτερον is not an adjective dependent on σημεῖον, but an adverb; in fact, it would be the whole complex τοῦτο πάλιν δεύτερον that would form an adverbial locution equivalent to τὸ δεύτερον. As for the noun σημεῖον, it would be the direct object of the verb ἐποίησεν. It would be necessary then to translate "A second (time), Jesus worked a sign...". But, if it is true that the formula πάλιν δεύτερον can have the sense of "a

47. See Blass-Debrunner, Grammatik[10], §§ 132, 1 and 292.
48. Less good are the translations of the Bible de Jerusalem: "Ce fut là un second signe que fit Jésus...", of the Traduction Œcuménique de la Bible: "Tel fut le second signe que Jésus accomplit...", or of R.E. Brown: "This was the second sign that Jesus performed...". The grammatical options remain the same however.
49. F. Neirynck, De semeia-bron in het vierde evangelie. Kritiek van een hypothese (Mededelingen van de Koninklijke Academie voor Wetenschappen, Letteren en Schone Kunsten van België), Brussels, 1983, pp. 14-15; E.T. in Evangelica II (BETL, 99), 1991, pp. 651-677.

second time" (cf. John 21:16), we shall see in regard to 21:14 that, contrary to the affirmations of Neirynck, in a formula such as τοῦτο δεύτερον the initial demonstrative always keeps its proper sense and cannot be assimilated to a simple article. And, since the evangelist himself has taken care to relate the two miracles of chapters 2 and 4 by recalling the wedding of Cana in 4:46a, the most normal procedure is to give the same grammatical structure to the two formulas of 2:11 and of 4:54.

2:1b, 11a	4:46a, 54a
...γάμος ἐγένετο	ἦλθεν οὖν πάλιν
ἐν Κανὰ τῆς Γαλιλαίας...	εἰς Κανὰ τῆς Γαλιλαίας
	ὅπου ἐποίησεν τὸ ὕδωρ οἶνον...
ταύτην (= τοῦτο) ἐποίησεν	τοῦτο δὲ πάλιν
ἀρχὴν τῶν σημείων	δεύτερον σημεῖον
ὁ Ἰησοῦς...	ἐποίησεν ὁ Ἰησοῦς...
...there was a wedding	He came then again
at Cana in Galilee...	to Cana in Galilee
	where he had changed water
	into wine...
This	This again
did Jesus as	did Jesus
the beginning of the signs...	as a second sign...

But, in the present structure of the gospel, one does not understand why these two "signs" are numbered. And why this importance given to the miracles done in Galilee, when Jesus had meanwhile done a great number of them in Jerusalem (2:23)? All is better understood if, in the source followed by the evangelist, these two miracles followed each other without interruption... and were followed by a third one which also was numbered. This is what we must demonstrate now.

DB. *The Third Miracle*

In its present context, the miracle of the miraculous draught of fish (21:1-14) would have been accomplished by Jesus after his resurrection. This fact is emphasized, both by the precise details given at the end of verse 14 "...brought back from the dead", and by the title "the Lord" given to Jesus (21:7, 12; cf. 20:18, 20, 25, 28). The gospel tradition does not know of other miracles that Jesus would have done after his resurrection; we are faced with a unique case, and which consequently poses a problem in itself. According to Spitta, Fortna, Heekerens[50], this miracle would have been done by Jesus during his earthly life, at the beginning of his ministry, and would be the third of a series beginning with the miracles of Cana and of Capharnaum of which we have just spoken. Fortna thus completes the *Semeia-Quelle* of Bultmann. With some nuances, and without accepting Bultmann's signs-source, this is the position that we are now going to defend.

1. *A Document Used by John and by Luke*

a) The story of the miraculous draught of fish, told in John 21:1-14, is not homogenous. It comprises two distinct events: the draught of fish, properly so called (vv. 1-4, 6, 8, 11) and a meal consisting of bread and grilled fish that Jesus offers to his disciples (vv. 9, 12-13). These two episodes are not intrinsically tied together, in the sense that, after verse 9, Jesus had already prepared *the* grilled fish that is going to constitute the repast of the disciples (v. 13). It is not a question of cooking and eating the fishes that were from the miraculous draught. A stylistic detail moreover permits us to think that the connection between the two episodes is artificial, and hence, secondary. In order to say "fish" Greek has at its disposal two different words: ἰχθύς and ὄψον; the latter is used most often in its diminutive form ὀψάριον. But ὄψον, or its diminutive, has a very precise sense: it designates fish that is ready to be eaten, which had either been cooked, or had been dried[51]. Contrary to the Synoptics, who only use the word ἰχθύς, the fourth gospel distinguishes carefully between the two terms. Fish that have just been caught and are thus still alive are designated by the word ἰχθύς (21:6, 8, 11) while fish prepared to be eaten are designated by the word ὀψάριον (6:9-11; 21:9, 13). But an exception to this rule exists: 21:10. In this verse, Jesus says to his disciples: "Now bring some of the fish that you have just caught". The fish had just been pulled out of the water, and still they are designated by the term ὀψάριον, which is

---

50. F. Spitta, *op. cit.*, pp. 68-70. R.T. Fortna, *The Gospel of Signs. A Reconstruction of the Narrative Source Underlying the Fourth Gospel* (SNTS Monograph Series 11), 1970, pp. 103-104. H.P. Heekerens, *Die Zeichen-Quelle der johanneischen Redaktion*, Heidelberg, 1978. For this last author, the three "signs", taken from a separate source, would have been added by the Redactor of the gospel.

51. Cf. Liddell and Scott: cooked or otherwise prepared food, a made dish, eaten with bread and wine.

abnormal (contrast v. 11). In another respect, this verse awkwardly tries to establish a connection between the two parts of the narrative, as if the disciples had to eat the fish that they had just caught, when in fact they only ate the fish prepared by Jesus (v. 13). One can therefore say that this v. 10 is redactional. At the same time that it unites two accounts originally distinct: an account of a miraculous draught of fish and an account of a post-Easter meal; the Redactor wanted to make an artificial tie between the two by adding v. 10.

b) This conclusion is confirmed by a reference to the gospel of Luke. There we read, in a separated state, on the one hand, an account of a miraculous catch of fish (5: 1-11) and on the other hand an account of a post-Easter meal (24: 41-43). The majority of commentators today recognize that the story of the miraculous catch of fish composed by Luke and John's version of it refer to one and the same event[52]. Moreover, in spite of the obvious differences, the post-Easter meal narrated by Luke and by John offers some significant contacts: it is a matter of eating dried fish, and above all, Jesus there asks the same question: "Have you something to eat?" (Luke 24: 41 and John 21: 5, with a somewhat different vocabulary).

In fact, we find ourselves confronted with a series of stories common to Luke and John; these are the main ones[53]:

Miraculous catch: Luke 5: 1-11 and John 21: 1-4, 6-8, 11
Peter comes to the tomb: Luke 24: 12 and John 20: 3-10
Apparition to the disciples gathered in Jerusalem: Luke 24: 36-39 and John 20: 19-20
Meal of dried fish: Luke 24: 41-43 and John 21: 5, 9, 12-13

We sense the existence of an archaic document on which Luke and John depended. This document contained an account of the miraculous catch. But Luke places the episode at the beginning of

---

52. Cf. Rudolf Pesch, *Der reiche Fischfang*, Dusseldorf, 1969.

53. In the following sequence, the authenticity of Luke 24: 12, omitted by the Western text, has been disputed. This verse contains in any case undeniable Lucan notes: see Benoit-Boismard, *Synopse des quatre évangiles*, tome II, 1972, pp. 445-446. Further, F. Neirynck, "Le récit du tombeau vide dans l'évangile de Luc (Lc 24,1-12)", in *Miscellanea in honorem Josephi Vergote* (Orientalia Lovaniensia Periodica, 6/7, 1975/1976), p. 427. Against the objections made to the authenticity of the verse, see J. Muddiman, "A Note on Reading Luke xxiv.12", *ETL* 48 (1972) 542-548. Also, F. Neirynck, "The Uncorrected Historic Present in Lk. xxiv.12", *ibid.*, 548-553. We note in passing this sentence of Neirynck's: "It is a now widely accepted view among defenders of the Lukan authenticity that there was a common source of John and Luke" (p. 548). As for Neirynck himself, he thinks that John 20: 3-10 depends on Luke 24: 12. See now his article in this sense: "ΑΠΗΛΘΕΝ ΠΡΟΣ ΕΑΥΤΟΝ, Lc 24,12 et Jn 20,10", *ETL* 54 (1978) 104-118.

Jesus' ministry, while John makes it a post-Easter event. How was it in their common source? An analysis of the Johannine source is going to invite us to agree with Luke against John.

2. *The Manifestation of the Messiah*

In the source used by John, the miraculous catch was not a post-Easter event; its aim was to portray the *manifestation* of Jesus, at the beginning of his ministry, *as the Messiah sent by God*. This could be deduced from the vocabulary used in vv. 1 and 14 to introduce and conclude the account: "After that, Jesus *manifested himself* (ἐφανέρωσεν ἑαυτόν) again to his dsiciples on the banks of the sea of Galilee. He revealed himself (ἐφανέρωσεν) thus" (v. 1) — "It is now the third (time that) Jesus *was manifested* (ἐφανερώθη) to his disciples..." (v. 14). The stress on the verb "to manifest", at the beginning and at the end of the account, is certainly deliberate[54]. Now, in the synoptic and Johannine tradition, this verb is nowhere else used to speak of the apparitions of the risen Christ[55]. When they want to speak of these apparitions, the verb used is always "to see" (ὁρᾶν). The Christ "had been seen" (ὤφθη) (1 Cor 15:5-8; Luke 24:34; Acts 13:31; cf. Acts 9:17; 26:16). He "would be seen" (ὄψεσθε, ὄψονται) by the disciples in Galilee (Matt 28:7, 10). The disciples rejoice (John 20:20) or doubt (Matt 28:17) "having seen" (ἰδόντες) the Lord. Finally, one who speaks of an apparition of the Risen One says "I saw" (ἑώρακα) the Lord (1 Cor 9:1; John 20:18, 25; cf. 20:29). The risen Christ is like the beings come from heaven and who "have been seen" by men (Luke 1:11; 22:43; Acts 2:3; 7:2, 30; 16:9; Rev 11:19; 12:1, 3; Matt 17:3 and par.). He became a being who belongs to the heavenly world, and, when He appeared on earth, the same vocabulary is used to describe him as for all the heavenly beings: he was "seen" (cf. already Gen 12:7; 17:1; 18:1; Exod 3:2 and *passim*).

On the other hand, the verb "to manifest" is almost a technical term, in Jewish literature and in the fourth gospel, to speak of the "manifestation" of the Messiah as Messiah, the moment he is going to begin his ministry. This theme is well known in Jewish tradition.

54. Ordinarily this verb is attributed to the evangelist on the pretext that it would be typically "Johannine". But we think that John 1:31; 2:11; 7:4; 21:1, 14 stem from the source used by the evangelist. See our further developments.
55. Mark 16:12, 14 are the only exception, but the text is a late one.

The Messiah must remain unknown to men up to the day he would be manifested as such, either by an action of God, or by the prophet Elijah returned to earth for this purpose. That means that, up until the day of his manifestation, the Messiah did not have any trait which could distinguish him from other men; he was "like everybody else". Consequently, God had to "manifest" him to mankind, as Messiah, in one way or another. This theme is set forth by Justin in his Dialogue with Trypho. He has the latter say: "Now the Christ, assuming that he is born and that he is somewhere, is unknown (ἄγνωστος). He himself does not know who he is and has no power, until Elijah comes to anoint him and to make him manifest (φανερόν) to all" (Dial 8:4). And again: "Even if they say that (the Christ) has come, it is not known who he is. But when he would be manifest (ἐμφανής) and glorious, then it will be known who he is" (110:1). But the theme is already attested in the first century before our era in the Psalms of Solomon, although in a less clear fashion: "May God cleanse Israel, for the day of mercy in blessing, for the appointed day, the time of the presentation (ἐν ἀνάξει) of his Christ" (18:5).

It is exactly this theme which John 1:26, 31 supposes. The Baptist begins by affirming to the Jews: "In your midst is one whom you do not know...". He will add later[56]: "And (even) I did not know him, but the reason why I came baptizing with water was *that he might be made known* (ἵνα φανερωθῇ) to Israel". Jesus is there, but nothing allows us to say that he is the Messiah sent by God. John the Baptist himself did not know that he had to be the Messiah. But God gave him a sign: the descent of the Holy Spirit (1:32-33), and he can present him to all as the "Chosen One" (1:34). This is the Jewish theme of the Messiah hidden and manifest[57], the Baptist holding the role of Elijah *redivivus* of Jewish tradition.

Outside of 21:1, 14, John's gospel contains two other passages, and two only, where the verb "to manifest" is said of Christ. The first forms the conclusion of the account of the wedding feast at Cana: "This Jesus did as a beginning of the signs at Cana in Galilee, and *he manifested his glory*" (καὶ ἐφανέρωσεν τὴν δόξαν αὐτοῦ; 2:11). This text is situated in the line of 1:31: Jesus was "made

---

56. In the source which the evangelist is following, vv. 26 and 31 would have followed immediately upon one another; Boismard-Lamouille, *Synopse* III, pp. 80ff.

57. See too, but only in the negative, John 7:27.

manifest" as the one sent from God, first by the Baptist, then by the first "sign" which he accomplished at Cana in Galilee. One should note the literary connection with the word of Trypho cited earlier: "when he will become manifest and glorious" (ἐμφανὴς καὶ ἔνδο-ξος). The second text is 7:3-4. the brothers of Jesus urge him to transfer his activity from Galilee to Judea, "so that your disciples also may see the works you are doing. No one works in secret if he wants to be known publicly. If you do these things, *manifest yourself* (φανέρωσον σεαυτόν) to the world". We will come back to this important text later. But the basic theme is clear: if Jesus wishes to manifest himself as Messiah, he must perform his miracles, no longer only in Galilee, but in Judea, the religious center of Judaism.

If we return to the account of the miraculous catch of fishes, one conclusion becomes evident. The point of this miracle is to "manifest" Jesus (vv. 1 and 14). In the source used by John, it was not an account of the appearance of the risen Christ: nowhere in it do the disciples say "they saw" Jesus, in accordance with the fourth evangelist's manner of speaking (1:35; 2:11; 7:4), it has to be a matter of the "manifestation" of Jesus as Messiah, as sent by God. This miracle is placed in the same line as that of the wedding at Cana, where Jesus "manifested His glory" (2:11).

3. *The Three Similar Formulas*

a) This conclusion is confirmed by an analysis of the formula which ends the account of the miraculous catch, analogous to the formulas which end the accounts of the first two "signs" performed by Jesus at Cana and at Capharnaum. Here are the three formulas:

2:11   ταύτην ἐποίησεν ἀρχὴν τῶν σημείων ὁ Ἰησοῦς... καὶ ἐφανέρωσεν τὴν δόξαν αὐτοῦ...
4:54   τοῦτο δὲ πάλιν δεύτερον σημεῖον ἐποίησεν ὁ Ἰησοῦς...
21:14   τοῦτο ἤδη τρίτον ἐφανερώθη Ἰησοῦς τοῖς μαθηταῖς...

2:11   Jesus did this as the beginning of his signs and so manifested his glory
4:54   This was the second sign Jesus did...
21:14   This was now the third time Jesus was made manifest to his disciples... [60].

---

58. In the hypothesis which we are going to propose, 4:54b and 21:14b would obviously come from the evangelist.

These three formulas begin with a desmonstrative pronoun, identical in 4:54 and 21:14, almost identical in 2:11 since, we have seen, the ταύτην is equivalent to a τοῦτο drawn to the gender of its antecedent. They involve a continuous enumeration: beginning, second, third. Jesus is the subject of the phrase. In addition, 2:11 and 4:54 contain the same expression "to work or do signs"; 2:11 and 21:14 have the same verb "to manifest", it being understood that Jesus *manifested himself by the signs* which he accomplished. Such formulas are not found elsewhere in the fourth gospel.

Neirynck[59], in order to dissociate as much as possible these three formulas, has contested the translation usually given by suggesting that the initial τοῦτο did not have the force of a demonstrative but equalled a simple article, as if one had had only τὸ τρίτον (cf. John 21:17; Mark 14:41). In order to support this hypothesis, he refers to texts such as Num 22:28, 32, 33; 24:10; Judg 16:15; 2 Cor 12:14; 13:1; or again to Gen 27:36; Num 14:22. In profane literature he refers to Herodotus, *Hist.* V:76. But *none* of these examples prove that the Greek demonstrative was equivalent to a simple article. In all the examples taken from the OT the Greek demonstrative translates a Hebrew demonstrative זה שלש רגלים or זה שלש פעמים. As for the Greek language, the dictionary of Liddell and Scott carefully distinguishes between the two formulas: τρίτον = a third time, but τοῦτο τρίτον = *this* third time; the authors underline the demonstrative and refer precisely to Num 22:32 and to John 21:14! In 2 Cor 13:1 (cf. 12:14), we must not translate "I come to you a third time", or "the third time", but as in RNAB, "This third time I am coming to you...". Let us return to the translation of Herodotus, *Hist.* V:76, given in the Guillaume Bude series[60]:

τέταρτον δὴ τοῦτο ἐπὶ τὴν Ἀττικὴν ἀπικόμενοι Δωριέες

"this was the fourth time that the Dorians came to Attica"

There is thus no reason, in John 21:14a, to conjure away the initial demonstrative and to abandon the translation usually given:

This was the third time that Jesus was made manifest... (BJ; cf. TOB)
Now *this* was the third time that... (R. Brown)
Dies das dritte Mal war, dass... (Haenchen)

---

59. *Op. cit.*, pp. 12-13.
60. Text established by P.E. Legrand.

Therefore we have three similar phrases which serve as conclusion to the three "signs" done by Jesus: changing the water into wine at Cana in Galilee (2:11), the healing of the royal official's son at Capharnaum (4:54a) and the miraculous catch of fish in the Sea of Galilee (21:14). At Cana, this was the "beginning" of the signs intended to manifest the glory of Jesus, and to designate him as the Messiah; at Capharnaum, this was the second sign; at the Sea of Galilee, this was the third time that Jesus manifested himself as Messiah. Such were the three signs which Jesus did at the beginning of his ministry in Galilee, according to the source taken up by the evangelist.

4. *A Displaced Text*

There remains a last problem to resolve pertaining to the third "sign" done by Jesus at the beginning of his ministry, as is again the case in Luke. Inevitably the question arises: why did the evangelist feel the need to transfer the episode and make of it an account of the appearance of the risen Christ? The answer is perhaps given by the fondness of the evangelist for number symbolism.

First let us give some examples. In John 4:16-18, Jesus reproaches the Samaritan woman for having had five husbands; now, in these three verses, the word "husband" (ἀνήρ) occurs five times. In 6:5-13, in the account of the multiplication of the loaves, it is a question of five loaves and two fishes; now, the word "bread" (ἄρτος) is used five times (vv. 5, 7, 9, 11, 13) and the word "fish" (ὀψάριον) two times (vv. 9 and 11). Seven disciples are going to take part in the miraculous catch of fish (21:2); now, in this account (21:1-14), the word "disciple" (μαθητής) is used seven times (vv. 1, 2, 4, 7, 8, 12, 14). This account echoes that of the calling by Jesus of the two disciples of the Baptist (1:35-37), with the same formula "two of his disciples" (1:35 and 21:2); now, in this little story, the word "disciple" occurs twice. This cannot be the effect of chance. The evangelist wants to stress certain words to indicate that they give the key to the narrative.

Among all these numbers, "seven" had a special importance well known in biblical and secular literature. It symbolized totality, perfection. In contrast, "six" was the symbol of imperfection since it lacked a unit to reach perfection. This double symbolism appears in the discourse of Jesus reported in John 5:31-47. Jesus there enumerates all those who bear witness to the reality of his mission, and the verb "to bear witness" appears seven times (vv. 31, 32, 33, 36, 37, 39) to symbolize the totality, fulness, perfection of the witnessings. But in spite of these testimonies, the Jews refuse to believe in Jesus; the verb "believe", always in the negative, turns up six times (vv. 38, 44, 46, 46, 47, 47). At the wedding in Cana, the stone urns containing water to be used for the purifications of the Jews number six (2:6); this number symbolizes that the system of purification of Judaism is imperfect, and thus out of date. It is replaced by the wine of the word brought by Christ (cf. 15:3). The gospel of John is marked by a succession of Jewish holidays: first Passover (2:13), Pentecost (?) (5:1), second Passover (6:4), Tabernacles (7:2), Dedication (10:22), third Passover (11:55). They are six in number. But the last Passover is Christ's Passover (13:1) and it is mentioned, by itself, seven times (11:55, 55; 12:1; 13:1; 18:28, 39; 19:14). The intention is clear: the whole system of Jewish holidays is replaced by the Christian holy day par excellence, Easter, during which believers celebrate the resurrection of the one whom the Jewish authorities had put to death.

It is within this perspective that we could explain the transfer of the account of the miraculous catch. The evangelist had received from his sources a series of seven "signs" performed by Jesus: the water changed into wine (2:1-11), the healing of the royal official's son (4:46-54), the miracle of the fishes (21:1-14), the healing of the paralytic by the pool of Bezata (5:1-18), the multiplication of the loaves (6:1-15), the healing of the man born blind (9:1-41) and the raising of Lazarus (11:1-44). But for him, the "sign" par excellence performed by Jesus was the resurrection of his own body (2:19-21). If the evangelist kept during the early life of Jesus all the "signs" received from his sources, he would have obtained eight, thus one too many (since seven would indicate totality, perfection). Thus he transferred one of them to after the resurrection, as if it was "out of sequence". And he chose that of the miraculous catch which he could fuse with the account of the post-Easter meal offered by Jesus to his disciples, since fish were involved in it. We have seen that, in this account, the evangelist had added v. 10 which tries to make the link between the two episodes by playing on the theme of the "fishes".

DC. *Some Linking Verses*

We have seen above that the link between the first sign (Cana) and the second sign (Capharnaum) was formed by John 2:12: Jesus goes down to Capharnaum accompanied by his family and his disciples. Is it still possible to find the link which existed in the early document, between the second and the third signs? Jesus traveled throughout Galilee (7:1a). His brothers then invite him to travel to Judea and to perform there his "works" which he had performed in Galilee, so that he could reveal himself to the world there (7:3-4). But Jesus refuses and remains in Galilee (7:6, 9). Read again especially verses 3-4:

> So his brothers said to him: "Leave here and go to Judea, so that your disciples also may see the works you are doing. No one works in secret if he wants to be known publicly. If you do these things, manifest yourself to the world".

By "works", we must understand the miracles (5:20, 36; 10:25, 32-38; 14:10-12; 15:24); this term, used especially by Jesus, is synonymous with "signs". For this scene to make sense, it is necessary that Jesus had not yet performed any miracle in Judea. His brothers said to him: up until now, you have performed your extraordinary "works" in Galilee; but what is the religious importance of that country (1:46; 7:52)? If you wish to be recognized as a religious reformer, if you wish to have a real influence on the Jewish people, reveal yourself to the world by exercising your activity in Judea, the religious center of Judaism. Thus, as was well seen by Wellhausen and Spitta, then after them by Bultmann and Haenchen, these vv. 3-4 do not know texts such as John 2:23; 4:45 and 5:1ff, according to which Jesus would have already performed several miracles in Jerusalem. Bultmann then thinks that this passage had to belong to the *semeia-Source* and, with hesitation, he proposes to replace it between the account of the healing of the royal official's son (4:46ff) and that of the healing of the paralytic (5:1ff)[61]. The solution we propose is similar; but, in line with the previous developments, we make of this little passage the link between the second and third "signs" performed by Jesus in Galilee. Jesus is at Capharnaum in the company *of his brothers* and his disciples (2:12);

---

61. *Das Evangelium des Johannes*, p. 217, note 1.

there he performs the "sign" of the healing of the royal official's son (4: 46ff). Then he begins to circulate in Galilee (7: 1a); *his brothers* (7: 3a; cf. 2: 12) suggest to him then to make Judea the center of his religious activity in order to reveal himself to the world there (7: 3-4). But Jesus refuses and remains in Galilee (7: 6, 9) where he is going to reveal himself as the Messiah thanks to his third "sign"; the miraculous catch (21: 1ff).

One might object that verse 3 supposes that Jesus had already made disciples in Judea. Haenchen, who has well seen the difficulty, proposes to see in the words "your disciples" an addition by the evangelist; the source simply had an impersonal plural: "... in order that the works which you do may be seen" (cf. 2: 23). This is possible, but perhaps not necessary. For the author of the older document was it possible that Jesus had had disciples in Judea even if he had never been there?

DD. *Jesus and Moses*

It is now possible for us to find again the parallelism between Jesus and Moses which runs all through the Gospel of John, especially in the story of the calling of Nathanael (1: 45-49), which precedes the account of the first "sign" performed by Jesus at Cana (2: 1-11) and is closely linked to it. The parallelism consists in this: just as, according to Exod 4: 1-9, Moses had to perform three "signs" in order to authenticate his mission to the Hebrews, so must Jesus himself perform three "signs" in Galilee in order to be "manifested" as the Messiah sent by God. This parallelism explains several particularities of the Johannine accounts. Before we show this, let us read the text of Exod 4: 1-9. God has just revealed himself to Moses, in the episode of the burning bursh, and entrusted him with a fearful mission: to deliver the Hebrew people from bondage in Egypt (3: 1-12). But Moses, little enthused by this mission, raises a series of objections (3: 12-22); finally, here is the dialogue which ensues between God and Moses:

(Exod 4: 1-9)

1 Then Moses answered, "But behold, they will not believe me or listen to my voice, for they will say, 'The Lord did not appear to you'".
2 The Lord said to him, "What is that in your hand?". He said, "A rod".

3   And he said, "Cast it on the ground". So he cast it on the ground, and
    it became a serpent; and Moses fled from it.
4   But the Lord said to Moses, "Put out your hand, and take it by the
    tail" — so he put out his hand and caught it, and it became a rod in
    his hand —
5   "that they may believe that the Lord, the God of their fathers, the God
    of Abraham, the God of Isaac, and the God of Jacob, has appeared to
    you".
6   Again, the Lord said to him, "Put your hand into your bosom". And
    he put his hand into his bosom; and when he took it out, behold, his
    hand was leprous, as white as snow.
7   Then God said, "Put your hand back into your bosom". So he put his
    hand back into his bosom; and when he took it out, behold, it was
    restored like the rest of his flesh.
8   "If they will not believe you", God said, "or heed the first sign, they
    may believe the latter sign.
9   If they will not believe even these two signs or heed your voice, you
    shall take some water from the Nile and pour it upon the dry ground;
    and the water which you shall take from the Nile will become blood
    upon the dry ground".

It is not a question of establishing an equivalence de facto of the
"signs" performed by Moses and those done by Jesus at the start of
his ministry. At most, one could compare the changing of water to
blood by Moses (Exod 4:9) to the "sign" of water changed to wine
by Jesus (John 2:1ff), and note that, for Jesus as well as for Moses,
the second sign consists of a healing. But we would like to show
rather how three particularities in the Johannine accounts of John
can be explained by referring to the text of Exodus.

a) In the account of Exodus, the miracles which Moses must do
are called "signs", in the Hebrew text (אות) as well as in the
Septuagint Greek (σημεῖον). They must, in effect, constitute the
"signs" that Moses had indeed been sent by God. Just so in the
gospel of John: the miracles of the water changed into wine and of
the healing of the royal official's son are "signs" (2:11 and 4:54).
This manner of designating miracles is moreover current in this
gospel[62]. On the other hand, in the Synoptics, the term most often
used is "powers" (δυνάμεις; Matt 7:22; 11:20-23; 13:54, 58; 14:2;
Mark 6:2, 5; 6:14; 9:39; Luke 10:13; 19:37). The word σημεῖον is
only found in the case of the "sign" coming from heaven for which
the Pharisees ask and which Jesus refuses to perform (Matt 12:38-39

62. John 2:23; 3:2; 6:2, 14, 26, 30; 7:31; 9:16; 10:41; 11:47; 12:18, 37; 20:30.

and par.; cf. Luke 23:8), and in the case of the false eschatological prophets (Matt 24:24 = Mark 13:22; cf. Deut 13:2-3). One can affirm therefore that, in the Synoptics, the miracles performed by Jesus are never called "signs". On this point John therefore represents a particularity that ties in to the manner of speaking of Exod 4:1-9.

b) In the Exodus story, the "signs" have above all an apologetic function: they must prove that Moses had indeed been sent by God. They are thus going to condition the faith of those who saw them, their faith in Moses' mission. This is said explicitly from the beginning of the account; the "signs" will have the aim of answering the objection which Moses raises: "But they will not believe me or listen to my voice, for they will say 'The Lord did not appear to you'" (4:1). And God will himself explain to Moses: "*If they do not believe you* and are not convinced by the first sign, *they will believe* because of the second sign. If *they do not believe*, even with these two signs..." (4:8-9). Thus the signs are for the purpose of permitting men to believe. This is exactly the Johannine perspective, clearly indicated in the first "sign": "Jesus did this as the beginning of *his signs* in Cana in Galilee, and so manifested his glory, and his disciples *believed in him*" (2:11). This theme of "signs", or of "works", which condition faith turns up often elsewhere in the gospel of John[63]. It is based on a very simple theology. A "sign" is a wonder which contradicts the laws of nature. But only God can break the laws of nature. Therefore when a man performs "signs", it is not he who is acting, but God who acts in him. This is the proof that "God is with him", and thus that he has been mandated by God (John 3:2; 9:31-33; cf. Exod 3:12).

But such is not the perspective of the Synoptics. To be sure, certain miracles evoke a Jesus who commands the forces of nature and obliges the disciples to ask themselves about his true personality, such as the miracle of the storm calmed: "Who is this that even the wind and the sea obey him?" (Mark 4:41 and par.). Similarly, in Matt 11:4-5 = Luke 7:21-23, Jesus gives the miracles which he has performed as proof that indeed he is "the one who is to come". But he makes it in implicit reference to Isa 61:1-4, and without insisting on the apologetic value of miracles; if Jesus is the one whom they

---

63. See John 2:23; 4:53; 11:42, 45; 12:11; 20:30-31; 10:37-38; 14:11.

waited, it is because he realized the prophetic oracles. In fact, when, in a narrative, the theme of faith is explicit, this is always prior to the miracle: it is not the miracle that conditions faith, but on the contrary faith that conditions the miracle. Put otherwise, it is necessary to believe already in order to benefit from the miracle. This theme is expressed in the stereotyped formula "Thy faith has saved thee" (Mark 5:34; 10:52; Matt 9:22; Luke 7:50; 8:48; 17:19; 18:42; cf. Matt 9:29; 15:28; Luke 7:9-10). Still on this point, the gospel of John distinguishes itself from the Synoptics[64] and goes back to the perspective of Exod 4:1-9.

c) There remains finally the problem of the numbering of the signs. In Exod 4:8-9 we have a first hint of an enumeration: "If they will not believe you, or heed the first sign, they may believe the latter sign. If they will not believe even these two signs...". Here already is the theme that will be systematized by the author of the early document taken up by the evangelist: "Jesus did this as the beginning of his signs" (2:11) — "This was the second sign Jesus did" (4:54) — "This was now the third time Jesus was revealed" (21:14). Fortna[65], who holds Bultmann's hypothesis concerning the *Semeia-Quelle*, and who does not make this relationship with Exod 4:8-9, asks himself why all the "signs" done by Jesus and mentioned in the fourth gospel are not numbered. He thinks that they were all numbered in the source, but that the evangelist has only kept the numbering of the first three. Our hypothesis is much more plausible: only the three signs worked by Jesus in Galilee at the beginning of his ministry were numbered, in reference to the three signs done by Moses according to Exod 3:1-9.

Fortna, followed by Heekerens, thinks that, in John 2:11, the Johannine source had, not "Jesus did this as the beginning of his signs", but "Jesus did this as first sign" (τοῦτο πρῶτον ἐποίησεν σημεῖον). The change would have been made by the disciple. We think so too. But we must add that the text proposed for the Johannine source is in fact attested by the following witnesses: "Epiphanius, Tatian, b (q) Syr[P] Sah Boh Eth". Does this textual tradition reflect the text of the source? Does it result from a correction made to harmonize the formula of 2:11 with that of

64. Cf. M.-É. Boismard, "Rapports entre foi et miracles dans l'évangile de Jean", *ETL* 58 (1982) 357-364.
65. *Op. cit.*, p. 105.

4:54? It is impossible to respond within the framework of the present study.

d) We have just seen how the reference to the theme of Jesus new Moses could explain certain traits through which the miracles recounted in the fourth gospel are distinguished from those that the synoptic gospels present, especially their designation as "signs" and their apologetic value. These conclusions are confirmed by the Acts of the Apostles. This book is the only one of the whole NT that applies explicitly to Jesus the text of Deut 18: 18-19 concerning the sending by God of a prophet like Moses (Acts 3: 22; cf. 7: 37). Now, contrary to synoptic usage, the miracle of the curing of the sick man lying at the Beautiful Gate of the Temple is called there "a sign" (4: 16, 22) as are the miracles done by Philip in Samaria (8: 6). And, as in the gospel of John, the miracles have an apologetic value; they lead to faith in Christ (8: 6; 9: 35, 42). It is indeed the same thematic that we meet occasionally in the Acts of the Apostles, and which has been systematized in the gospel of John.

E. *Synthesis*

We can now reconsider the gospel of John by taking into account the analyses we have made concerning the theme of Jesus, new Moses. By way of synthesis we shall see that a certain number of characteristics of the fourth gospel can be understood quite well within the perspective of this theme [66].

1. *Jesus is God's Emissary*

Every prophet has been sent by God in view of a determined mission. He only has authority over men in virtue of this mission that he has received from God. This is true in the first place of Moses. We recall simply two texts that we have had occasion to study previously. In Exod 3: 12 God says to Moses at the time when he invests him with his mission as liberator of the Hebrews: "I shall be with you and that shall be for you a sign that I sent you". Later,

---

66. The goal of this synthesis is to list a certain number of the fourth gospel's typical themes, without pursuing a fuller exegesis of them. We only want to show to how great an extent this gospel was written in close dependence on the theme of Jesus as new Moses.

during the Exodus, Moses will say to the Hebrews: "By this you will know that the Lord has sent me" (Num 16:28). To emphasize that Jesus is not only a prophet, but furthermore the prophet par excellence, the new Moses, the gospel of John has made conspicuous, more than all the other writings in the NT, the fact that Jesus has been sent by God.

a) To express the idea of sending, Greek has available two synonymous verbs: πέμπειν and ἀποστέλλειν. The first of these verbs is used in the gospel of John in a quite exceptional fashion. We find it twenty five times under an almost stereotyped form. Jesus speaks of God or of his Father, referring to him by the expression "the one who sent me" (ὁ πέμψας με)[67]. So, for the Johannine Christ, one of the essential relations that exist between the Father and him is that of the Sender and the Sent. The importance of this fact is underlined by noting that, in the synoptic gospels, we only find the same verb once to signify the mission of Jesus, and that in an indirect fashion, in the parable of the murderous laborers in the vineyard (Luke 20:13)[68]. Note further that, in this parable, Jesus is, chronologically speaking, only the last of a series of messengers. In the gospel of John, on the contrary, Jesus is "the Messenger" par excellence, since he defines God in reference to this mission that he had received from him.

b) The use of the verb ἀποστέλλειν is less characteristic of John, but still keeps a special significance. In the gospel of John it is said sixteen times that God has sent Jesus into the world[69]. To be sure, the same verb is used for others besides Jesus, like the Baptist for example (John 1:6; 3:28); but John the Baptist was a prophet. It remains that its frequency in regard to Jesus is remarkable enough. In the Synoptics, it is much less strong[70].

c) In order to signify the mission of Jesus by God, the disciples also often use the verb "to come". The equivalence between "I have come" and "I have been sent" is very clear if one compares for example John 12:46-47 to 3:17. To be sure, of the Baptist too one can say that he came, sent by God (1:7). But it is especially in

---

67. John 1:33; 4:34; 5:23, 24, 30, 37 and *passim*.
68. Matthew and Mark have a different verb that we will look at later.
69. John 3:17, 34; 5:36, 38; 6:29, 57 and *passim*.
70. Matt 10:40 and par.; 15:24; 21:37 and Mark 12:2; Luke 4:43.

regard to Jesus that this verb is used in the transcendent sense[71]. To evaluate the importance of the theme of the mission of Jesus by God, we must then take into account also this verb "to come", even if one finds it often enough in the Synoptics with an analogous sense.

d) Let us point out finally, last but not least, the negative correlative of the theme of the sending of Jesus by God: he does nothing of himself; everything he does is in virtue of the mission that he has received from God. This theme, we have said, has its origin in Num 16:28 in which text Moses says: "By this you will know that the Lord has sent me to do all these things that (I do not do) on my own". The tie with the theme of the mission is very clear in John 7:28-29: "Yet I did not come on my own, but the one who has sent me, whom you do not know, is true. I know him, because I am from him, and he sent me". The reference to Num 16:28 is clearer in John 8:28-29: "When you lift up the Son of Man, then you shall know that I am, and that I do nothing on my own, but I say only what the Father has taught me. The one who sent me is with me". As the prophet announced through Deut 18:18, Jesus does not speak on his own, he only transmits the words that God has put in his mouth. This theme that Jesus does not do anything on his own is frequent in the fourth gospel[72]; it is never found in the synoptic gospels.

We can then say that, under one form or another, the gospel of John has as its background the idea that, if Jesus came, it is because he has been vested by God with a special mission. The exceptional importance of this theme comes, without any doubt, from the fact that Johannine Christology has as its foundation the certitude that Jesus is the Prophet like Moses announced by Deut 18:18-19.

2. The Purpose of his Mission

But why was Jesus sent by God? Above all to transmit to us his Words. The prophet is the one who speaks in the name of God. In an imageful and rather anthropomorphic manner, God says to Moses when he vests him with his mission, "I will be with your mouth and teach you what you shall speak" (Exod 4:12). Or, as the Septuagint translates, "I shall put my word in your mouth". The

---

71. John 6:14, as the prophet like Moses; cf. 1:9, 15; 3:2, 19, 31; 5:43; and *passim.*
72. Cf. John 5:19, 30; 7:17-18; 8:42; 14:10.

prophet is like the mouth of God. So too the prophet like Moses announced by Deut 18:18 will respeak to men everything that God will command him to say. We have seen that this basic theme had been taken up in John 12:49-50: "I did not speak on my own, but the Father who sent me commanded me what to say and speak... So what I say, I say as the Father told me". And the same in 8:28: "I do nothing on my own, but I say only what the Father taught me. The one who sent me is with me". When Jesus speaks it is not his word that he gives us, but that of the Father (cf. 17:8, 14); it is as if the Father himself were speaking to us (cf. 14:10).

This theme recurs repeatedly again in the gospel, under different forms. Thus Jesus said to his disciples: "Whoever does not love me does not keep my words; yet my word is not mine[73], but that of the Father who sent me" (14:24). He said the same to the Jews: "My teaching is not my own but is from the one who sent me. Whoever chooses to do his will shall know whether my teaching is from God or whether I speak on my own" (7:16-17).

Thus, when the Johannine Christ makes references to his teaching, to his words, he expresses himself as Moses himself would have done to affirm the perfect identity between what he tells us and what God wants to tell us through his mouth.

3. *The Proofs that Jesus is God's Envoy*

But what proofs have we that it is indeed so, and that Jesus speaks to us as if God himself were speaking? To answer that question, let us go back once more to the precedent of Moses.

a) To authenticate his mission to the Hebrews, God gives him a staff thanks to which he can work a certain number of extraordinary actions that the biblical narrative calls "signs" (Exod 4:1-9); so too, of Jesus.

When the evangelist speaks of these miracles, he calls them signs. The first of these signs worked by Jesus is the changing of water into wine at Cana; the disciple ends his account by noting: "Jesus did this as the beginning of his signs... and so revealed his glory, and his disciples began to believe in him" (John 2:11). The miracle has as its

---

73. This is the reading of the Western text. The other witnesses read: "the word which you hear"; this is a facilitating reading to avoid the apparent contradiction: "and my word is not mine".

goal the awakening of the faith of those present. The last of the signs that Jesus worked during his earthly life is the resurrection of Lazarus (cf. 11:47). Before accomplishing it, Jesus said a prayer to his Father so that it would be clear that this resurrection was coming from God. Jesus had never doubted it, but if he proclaims it before all, it is so that all may believe that he has been sent by the Father (11:41-42). If the crowds follow Jesus, it is because of the signs that he works before them (John 6:2). These same crowds, having seen the miracle of the multiplication of the loaves, recognize that Jesus is truly "the Prophet who comes into the world", that is, the Prophet like Moses announced in Deut 18:18.

When Jesus speaks of miracles, he calls them "works", in reference no longer to Exod 4:1-9 but to Num 16:28. More clearly than the evangelist, in view of the incredulity of the Jews he underlines the apologetic value of the works that he accomplishes. After the curing of the paralytic, he said to them: "The works that the Father gave me to accomplish, these works that I perform testify on my behalf that the Father has sent me" (5:36). During the feast of the Dedication, the Jews ask him to tell them clearly if he is the Christ. And Jesus answers: "I told you and you do not believe. The works I do in my Father's name testify to me" (10:25). He will insist a little later: "If I do not perform my Father's works, do not believe me. But if I do them, even if you do not believe me, believe the works, so that you may know and recognize that the Father is in me and I am in the Father" (10:37-38). The works witness then that Jesus has indeed been sent by the Father.

Note that Jesus traces to God the miraculous power that acts in him and through him (cf. also 11:41-42). This is precisely what gives the miracles an apologetic value. A man cannot break the laws of nature; God alone can do it. If then a man performs miracles, it is that God acts in him, it is that God recognizes him as his messenger. This is what Nicodemus well understood when he said to Jesus: "Rabbi, we know that you are a teacher who has come from God, for no one can do these signs that you are doing unless God is with him" (3:2; cf. Exod 3:12). The man born blind, cured by Jesus, understood it well too. He explains to the unbelieving Jews: "It is unheard of that anyone ever opened the eyes of a man born blind. If this man (Jesus) were not from God, he would not be able to do anything" (9:32-33).

b) It is not only the signs or the works that give evidence of Jesus' mission, there are also the words that he transmits to men. The message that Jesus brings to us is so engaging that it can only come from God.

This apologetic value of the Word is sometimes compared with that of the works as in this text of the discourse after the Supper: "If I had not come and spoken to them, they would have no sin; but as it is, they have no excuse for their sin... If I had not done works among them that no one else ever did, they would no have sin; but as it is, they have seen and hated both me and my Father" (15: 22-24). This comparison between words and works makes one think of the story of Moses' call in Exod 4: 1-17. God gives him first to work the signs that must accredit his mission (4: 1-9). Then he explains that he will be with his mouth to teach him what he must say (4: 10-12). The whole is summed up at the end of the episode: "I will be with your mouth and with his mouth (Aaron's), and will teach you what you shall do... And you shall take in your hand this rod, with which you shall do the signs" (4: 15-17).

But the apologetic value of the Word is sometimes also opposed to that of the signs[74]. In John 4: 48 Jesus reproaches the royal official of Capharnaum with having need of signs and of marvels in order to believe (cf. 20: 29). Upon what then can men base their faith? The evangelist indicates it at the end of the episode of the conversation of Jesus with the Samaritan woman. She had sensed that Jesus must be the Christ because he had proven that he was acquainted with the facts of her private life, and thus that he possessed a supernatural knowledge of beings (4: 16-19, 29). This was to perform a sort of sign. The woman succeeds then in convincing the people of her village who flock to Jesus (4: 30); they believe by basing themselves on the testimony of the woman announcing that Jesus has taken her to task for all her past as a perverse woman (4: 39). Jesus then spends two days in the village, and the disciple concludes: "And they believed in great numbers, because of his word, and they said to the woman, 'We no longer believe because of your word; for we have heard for ourselves, and we know that this is truly the savior of the world'" (4: 41-42). So too, when Jesus had pronounced his bread of life discourse, the

---

74. On this problem, see the fuller developments in M.-É. Boismard, "Rapports entre foi et miracle dans l'évangile de Jean", *ETL* 58 (1982) 357-364.

majority of his disciples abandon him in spite of the miracle of the multiplication of the loaves that they had seen just previously (6:60-66). But the twelve stay with Jesus, and Peter gives the reason: "Lord, to whom shall we go? You have the words of eternal life" (6:68). The twelve remain with Jesus, not because they had seen the signs and marvels, but because they had learned that the words of Jesus are words of life. These words have, by themselves, the power to convince men that they come from God.

We must recognize, in any case, that these last developments have nothing that could evoke, at least directly, the theme of the Prophet like Moses.

4. *Death and Life*

What is going to be the reaction of men faced with the words that the new Moses transmits to them from the side of God? They will either reject or accept these words.

a) If they reject them, they incur a condemnation. This was the theme expressed in Deut 18:19, read according to a targum: "The man who does not listen to what the Prophet will tell them in my name, my word will demand an account of him". This theme, one has seen, is taken up in John 12:48: "Whoever rejects me and does not accept my words has something to judge him: the word that I spoke, it will condemn him on the last day". This theme of the judgment of condemnation holds a great place in the gospel of John. In certain passages, it is a matter of a judgment that will take place at the end of time (John 12:47-48; 5:21-23, 27-29). In others, the judgment is already realized, according to whether men accept or reject the message of Christ (3:17-21; 12:31).

b) But if men accept the word of Christ, they will obtain eternal life. This theme of eschatological life is especially typical of the gospel of John since it turns up there 36 times, while it is only found 14 times in the three Synoptics. Now we can link it up without difficulty to the theme of the new Moses. We have seen as a matter of fact that John 12:48-50 formed a chiasm constructed on the basis of texts from Deut 18:18-19 and Num 16:28. Now we read in the center of this chiasm: "and I know that his commandment is life eternal". The idea is then that man obtains eternal life by obeying the words that the new Moses transmits to us from God. Look at the text of Deut 32: 44-47. After the reading of the law that Moses has transmitted to the Hebrews from God, the prophet exhorts them to observe it, and he ends with these words: "This law is no trifle for you, but it is your life, and thereby you shall live long in the land which you are going over the Jordan to possess". The Hebrews will only live, as people, in the measure that they keep the Word of God transmitted by Moses. The implicit idea is that they will die the day they reject this Word.

This theme had been developed in Deut 30: 15-20 (LXX):

> Behold, I have set before you this day *life and death*, good and evil. If you will hearken to the commands of the Lord your God, which I command you this day... then you shall live and be many in number... But if your heart change, and you will not hearken, and you will go astray and worship other gods, and serve them, I declare to you this day that you will utterly perish... I call both heaven and earth to witness this day against you, I have set before you *life and death*, the blessing and the curse: choose life, that you and your seed may live: to love the Lord your God, to hearken to his voice, and to cleave to him; for this is your life...

So too, in the gospel of John, he who listens to the word of Christ, the messenger of God, the new Moses, has chosen life: "Whoever hears my word and believes in the one who sent me has eternal life and will not come to condemnation, but has passed from *death to life*" (John 5: 24; cf. 1 John 3: 14). The perspective is no longer collective, but individual. In spite of everything, how can we doubt that this Johannine text, recalling the mission of the Christ through God, does not refer implicitly to the text of Deut 30: 15-20?

We have passed in review a certain number of the most typical themes of John's gospel and we have seen that all of them ought to be connected more or less explicitly to the theme of Jesus new Moses, in reference especially to the texts of Deut 18: 18-19 and Num 16: 28. We can therefore affirm that this theme forms the background of the whole of the fourth gospel.

Conclusion

At the end of the first part of our inquiry, we can summarize its conclusions by recalling the road that we have covered. Nowhere, in the gospel of John, is the text of Deut 18: 18-19 cited explicitly with regard to Jesus. It is in any case certain that the theme of Jesus new Moses runs all through this gospel. It is evoked first by the title "the

Prophet" which is given to Jesus (6:14; 7:40, 52; cf. 1:21). Jesus is just not any prophet, but "the Prophet" who must come into the world (6:14). This Prophet can only be "the one of whom Moses has written in the law" (1:45; 5:46), that is, the prophet like Moses who God has promised to send in Deut 18:18-19. Rather than citing this text explicitly when applying it to Jesus, as in Acts 3:22, the evangelist preferred to proceed in a more subtle fashion, as Jeremiah had done previously. He puts in the mouth of Jesus words that are a copy, either of Deut 18:18-19, or of other texts of the Pentateuch concerning Moses, like Num 16:28; Exod 3:12, etc. Thus Jesus speaks as if it were Moses himself who was speaking (John 12:48-50; 8:28-29; 14:10; 7:16-17; 17:6, 8, 26).

The analysis of the narrative of the calling of Philip and of Nathaniel, in John 1:43-49, has permitted us to link up this theme, as it is expressed in the gospel of John, to Samaritan traditions. In vv. 45 and 49, in effect, Jesus is designated at the same time, implicitly as the Prophet like Moses announced in Deut 18:18, explicitly as "the son of Joseph" and "the king of Israel". Now, in the story of the wedding feast of Cana that follows immediately, the word of Mary to the waiters "Do everything he will tell you" is a quotation from Gen 41:55 where the same statement is made by the Pharaoh of Egypt in regard to the patriarch Joseph. Jesus is then, not only the Prophet like Moses, but also "the son of Joseph" in the dynastic sense that the expression can include: the heir of the royal prerogatives of the patriarch considered as the ancestor of the Samaritans. For the Samaritans, two figures of the OT dominate all the others: Moses the Prophet and Joseph the King. Jesus realized then in his person the eschatological aspirations of the Samaritan people[75].

We have finally been led to envisage the hypothesis of a Johannine source in which Jesus will have begun his ministry by accomplishing three miracles in Galilee: the water changed to wine at Cana (2:1-11), the son of a royal official cured at Capharnaum (4:46-54) and the miraculous haul of fish in the Sea of Galilee (21:1-14), a hypothesis held also by Spitta at the beginning of the century, then by Fortna and Heekerens. This hypothesis takes on its full meaning

75. In that case one could ask whether the Philip who becomes a disciple of Jesus in John 1:43 would not be identical with the Philip who would later evangelize Samaria according to Acts 8:5ff.

in the perspective of the fourth gospel: just as Moses had to do three
"signs" to prove to the Hebrews that he had indeed been sent by
God (Exod 4:1-9), so too Jesus would do three "signs" at the
beginning of his ministry to be able to be "manifested" as the
Prophet who had been promised by God in Deut 18:18-19.

CHAPTER TWO

JESUS IS THE WISDOM OF GOD

This chapter begins the harmonic variations on the fundamental theme: Jesus can fulfill the same role as Moses, and in a much better way, because he is the Wisdom of God come into the world.

1. *Wisdom*

a) Wisdom is "the perfect knowledge of all things that man can have" (Descartes). But this knowledge is not purely speculative, it is directed to action. If we want to act as we should, we have to know well the beings and things which surround us and upon which we more or less depend. Wisdom consists therefore in knowing all things so as to lead one's life rightly and, in so doing, to find as much happiness as possible.

Such wisdom may be simply human. In that case, it is acquired either by personal or collective experience, passed on from generation to generation. It may also come from heaven, given by God to human beings. ·In this sense, it is basically linked to the Spirit, it is the result of the presence in each one of us of the Spirit of God. Thus, speaking of the future Messiah, David's successor, Isaiah declares: "The Spirit of the Lord shall rest upon him, the *spirit of wisdom* and understanding, the spirit of counsel and might, the spirit of knowledge and the fear of the Lord" (Isa. 11:2). The Book of Wisdom echoes this oracle of Isaiah when it puts these words into the mouth of Solomon: "I prayed and was given understanding, I called upon God and the *spirit of Wisdom* came upon me" (Wis 7:7).

This wisdom sent by God is the source of all human knowing. Thanks to it Solomon can boast at having an "unfailing knowledge of creatures". He then indulges in reckoning the sum of the things he knows "... the structure of the world and the activity of the elements, the beginning, the end and the middle of time, the rotation of solstices, cycles of years, the positions of the stars, natures of animals and the instincts of wild beasts, powers of the winds and thoughts of men, uses of plants and virtues of roots. Whatever is hidden or visible have I known, for I was taught by Wisdom, the maker of all things" (Wis 7: 17-21).

But wisdom also enables us to know God's will for humanity. "Who indeed can know God's purpose and who can conceive what the Lord wants?... And who has known thy will if thou hast not given thy wisdom and sent down thy Holy Spirit?" (Wis 9: 13, 17). Thus Wisdom enables human beings to know the will of God, to live according to "God's pleasure" and so to obtain happiness. In the last text cited, you will have noted in passing the synonymous parallelism between the two last parts of the sentences which lead us to establish a quasi identity between Wisdom and the Spirit.

b) From the 5th century B.C. on, the Bible gave an exceptional importance to the theme of Wisdom, following the return from exile[1]. The books of wisdom make their appearance and then proliferate: Job, Proverbs, Ecclesiastes, Sirach, chapters 3 and 4 of the book of Baruch, the Wisdom of Solomon. Books which all claim to give men true knowledge of God's will. In this way, Wisdom tends to take the place of the Mosaic Law; more exactly, it becomes another expression of the Law. After having praised Wisdom and the favours it lavishes upon humanity, the author of Sirach adds: "All this is but the book of the Most High (God), the Law given by Moses, left as an inheritance to the congregations of Jacob" (Sir 24: 23). Likewise in the book of Baruch, the description of Wisdom ends with these words: "It is the book of God's instructions, the everlasting Law: whoever holds it shall live, whoever forsakes it shall die... Blessed are we, Israel, that which pleases God has been revealed to us" (Bar 4: 1-4).

In the Gospel of John, it was thus easy to pass from the theme of Jesus/Moses to that of Jesus/Wisdom. Jesus is the more entitled to being considered as the Prophet like Moses announced by Deut 18: 18 as he is the incarnate Wisdom of God. Not only has he, as Moses did, come to bring men, on behalf of God, the Law of the new covenant, but he himself *is* the Wisdom and Law which speaks to men to tell them how they have to act in order to please God. We now have to develop this point.

---

1. There is a good overview of wisdom literature in B.L. Mack, *Logos und Sophia. Untersuchungen zur Weisheitstheologie im hellenistischen Judentum* (Studien zur Umwelt des Neuen Testaments 10), 1973.

2. *Wisdom Must Come into this World*

The Sapiential books contain a certain number of almost stereo-typed sequences. In them Wisdom praises herself. She first states her relation to God. Then she summons up the part she played in the work of creation; after that she explains how she came among men and she lists the favours she has brought upon them.

a) The earliest of these texts appears in Prov 8:22–9:6[2]. There Wisdom first states her relation to God: she was created before the creation of the cosmos, she was begotten by God before the world was (8:22-26). Then comes a long account about the part she played in creation: she was standing by God, as if God sought her counsel to achieve the work of creation (8:27-30; cf. 3:19). In the end, she came to earth and "her delight was with the sons of men" (8:31). She can then invite men to listen to her counsels and become wise through her informed direction; it is for them a question of life or death (8:32-36; cf. 1:20-33; 3:20-21). Under another image, she invites them to come and share the banquet she has prepared, to eat her bread and drink her wine (9:1-6), symbols of the teaching she lavishes upon all those who wish to receive it.

b) In Sir 24:3-22, the structure of the sequence is more compli-cated, with the repetition of some themes. Wisdom first introduces herself as "coming from the mouth of the Most High" (24:3); a little later she will come back to her connection with God by saying that God created her "before the ages", therefore, before the creation of the cosmos (24:9). Her role in creation is described by way of her presence to all the elements of the world: the heavens, the abysses, the sea, the peoples (24:4-6). Finally, through God's order, she pitched her tent in Jacob and in Israel (24:8, 10-11) and there grew and spread her boughs like a prosperous vine (24:12-17). And there she invites men to come and satisfy themselves on her goods, to eat her bread and drink the beverage she offers to all (24:19-22; cf. 15:3); this is for them a question of life or death (cf. 4:11-19).

c) In Wis 7:22–9:18, the classical theme is found again, but this time in both a deeper and a more diffuse way. The relations of

2. See the detailed analysis of this text by Maurice Gilbert, "Le discours de la Sagesse en Proverbes, 8. Structure et cohérence", in *La Sagesse de l'Ancien Testament* (a collection of essays edited by M. Gilbert) (BETL 51), 1979, ²1990, pp. 202-218.

Wisdom with God are referred to from 7:26 on. She is "a refraction of eternal light, a stainless mirror of God's activity, an image of His goodness". She has shared in the work of creation (9:1-2); when God made the cosmos, she was with him, present at his side (9:9). That is why Solomon asks God to send it down from heaven so it can be with him and help him fulfill his job as a King (9:4, 10-12). The perspective broadens with verses 13-18: all men benefit from the blessing God's Wisdom is going to send upon them (v. 17); they will thus be able to know God's will, what pleases Him, act wisely and finally be saved (v. 18).

In all these texts Wisdom is almost personified. It appears as a person who, issuing from God, comes on earth to teach men the secrets of nature as well as the mysteries of the Divine Will. Now, this Wisdom, living among men, inviting them to come and "eat the bread of prudence and drink the water of wisdom" (Sir 15:3) is Jesus himself, the incarnation of Wisdom. John is going to show us this in a discreet but definite way.

3. *Jesus, Wisdom Made Man*

The very term of "Wisdom" does not appear in the Fourth Gospel. Nowhere does John explicitly say that Jesus is Wisdom. But to suggest it, he will use the literary method he already employed to show us how Jesus is the Prophet like Moses announced in Deut 18:18: he speaks of Jesus in the same way as the wisdom books speak of Wisdom; better still, he puts into Jesus' mouth the words uttered by Wisdom in the sapiential books.

a) The first half of the Prologue of the Gospel, speaking of the Word, takes up the scheme we have described above concerning Wisdom[3]. John first describes the relationship of the Word with God: from the beginning it was "with God", it was God (1:1-2). He then declares that it played a role in the work of creation (1:3-5). Then appear the different stages of its coming into the world (vv. 9-11). And last we learn the benefits it has brought to everyone who received it (vv. 12-13). We shall take up these texts in greater detail when we try to pin down in what sense Jesus is the Word of God.

---

3. Cf. Ceslas Spicq, "Le Siracide et la structure littéraire du Prologue de saint Jean", in *Mémorial Lagrange*, Paris, 1940, pp. 183-195.

But we can already understand how, for the evangelist, the Word which became flesh in Jesus (v. 14) is analogous to the Wisdom of God. Jesus is at once the Word and the Wisdom of God.

b) In his speech after the Last Supper Jesus says to his disciples: "Whoever has my commandments and observes them is the one who loves me. And whoever loves me will be loved by my Father, and I will love him and reveal myself to him" (14:21). Here Jesus speaks as Wisdom could do. Let us take up these sentences one by one and give their sapiential equivalent:

John 14:21	ὁ ἔχων τὰς ἐντολάς μου καὶ τηρῶν αὐτὰς ἐκεῖνός ἐστιν ὁ ἀγαπῶν με
Wis 6:18	ἀγάπη δε τήρησις νόμων αὐτῆς
John 14:21	Whoever has my commandments and observes them is the one who loves me
Wis 6:18	Love is the keeping of his laws

No doubt, the idea that love consists in keeping the commandments can first be said of God. One can read, for instance in Sir 2:15-16: "Those who fear the Lord do not transgress his words, and those who love him observe his ways. Those who fear the Lord seek how to please him, and those who love him feed upon his Law". But John's text is, in its literary form, nearer to the form in the book of Wisdom.

John 14:21	ὁ δὲ ἀγαπῶν με ἀγαπηθήσεται ὑπὸ τοῦ πατρός μου
Sir 4:14	τοὺς ἀγαπῶντας αὐτὴν ἀγαπᾷ ὁ κύριος
Wis 7:28	οὐθὲν γὰρ ἀγαπᾷ ὁ θεὸς εἰ μὴ τὸν σοφίᾳ συνοικοῦντα
John 14:21	whoever loves me will be loved by my Father
Sir 4:14	they that love it (Wisdom), the Lord loves them
Wis 7:28	the Lord only loves him who dwells with Wisdom
John 14:21	κἀγὼ ἀγαπήσω αὐτὸν
Prov 8:17	ἐγὼ τοὺς ἐμὲ φιλοῦντας ἀγαπῶ
John 14:21	(he that loves me) I will love him
Prov 8:17	I love those who love me
John 14:21	καὶ ἐμφανίσω αὐτῷ ἐμαυτόν
Wis 6:12	θεωρεῖται ὑπὸ τῶν ἀγαπώντων αὐτήν
John 14:21	I will reveal myself to him
Wis 6:12	it appears to those who love it.

Thus the Johannine text is a mosaic alluding to texts belonging to the sapiential books concerning those who love Wisdom. This is a discreet insinuation that Jesus is none other than Wisdom incarnate.

c) In John 3:12-13, Jesus says to his disciples: "If I tell you about earthly things and you do not believe, how will you believe if I tell you about heavenly things? No one has gone up (ἀναβέβηκεν) to heaven except the one who has come down from heaven, the Son of Man". This Johannine text has, as a background, two different thought related wisdom texts. The first, about the knowledge of earthly things and of heavenly things, is Wis 9:16-17: "Scarce do we guess *the things on earth*, and what is within our grasp we find with difficulty; but when *things are in heaven*, who can search them out? Or whoever knew your counsel, except you had given *Wisdom* and sent your holy spirit from on high?". Thus only Wisdom gives men the power of knowing the things of heaven, namely God's will.

The second text is Bar 3:29. In fact in verse 13 of the Johannine text the Greek perfect ἀναβέβηκεν cannot allude to the ascension of Jesus, since he is speaking and his ascension has not yet occurred. It is a durative perfect: Jesus nevers stops going up to heaven. And if he goes there, it is so that he can speak to us about the "heavenly things" alluded to in verse 12. The theme is expressed in Bar 3:29: "Who has gone up to the heavens and taken her (Wisdom) or brought her down from the clouds?". Because Jesus is Wisdom, he can, at any moment go up to heaven and bring down this wisdom needed by men so that they may know the "heavenly things".

d) The last text which we have to analyse is the call of the first disciples in John 1:35-51. But we must first note a problem of textual criticism.

da) At v. 1:41, four readings are in competition:

πρωτον	P⁶⁶ P⁷⁵ B a f l q Sah Boh Arm Geo
πρωτος	*N* Koine
πρωι	b e j r Syrˢ
omit	2148 Syrᶜ Aug

All of these readings may be explained by scribal errors. Let us put them back into their context:

ΟΥΤΟΣΠΡΩΤΟΝΤΟΝΑΔΕΛΦΟΝ

If the reading πρωτον is original, the variant πρωτος may be explained by the ουτος which comes before it; this case is classical. On the other hand, if the reading πρωτος is original, the variant πρωτον may be explained by the influence of the τον which comes after it; this case is equally a classical one. This reading πρωτος may equally explain the variant which omits this word; it may have fallen out by haplography, after ουτος. There remains the variant πρωι, which must be considered in function of the reading πρωτον. It seems that the passage from one reading to the other is easier if one supposes an original πρωι:

ΟΥΤΟΣΠΡΩΙΤΟΝΑΔΕΛΦΟΝ

There would have been the suppression of the *iota* and the dittography of the article τον. In the opposite case, we would have to suppose that one of the two τον fell out through haplography, which is quite possible, but also the creation of a new word, πρωι, by the addition of a *iota*, which becomes much more difficult. Let us add that, from the viewpoint of external criticism, and in the absence of Codex Bezae, we should neglect the agreement between the old Syriac version and the old African text, represented by the *Palatinus* (e). We shall return to this variant later on.

db) The narrative of the call of the first disciples is very stylized. It puts into play two themes attested elsewhere in the gospel. The first theme is that he who seeks Jesus must find him. It is already present in the Old Testament, either about God or about Wisdom[4]. Then in Isaiah 55: 6: "Seek the Lord while he may be found". And in the negative: "They shall go to seek the Lord, but they shall not find him" (Hosea 5: 6). And wisdom declares: "Those who seek me find me" (Prov 8: 17), or in the negative: "(The wicked) seek me but find me not" (Prov 1: 28). The second theme is that the disciple who follows Jesus must come to where Jesus is. Thus the Christ declares in John 12: 26: "Whoever serves me must follow me, and where I am, there also will my servant be" (John 12: 26; cf. 14: 3; 17: 24).

These two themes are united, but in the negative, in John 7: 34, in regard to the Jews who represent the anti-disciples, those who will not believe. Jesus says to them: "Ye will look for me but not find me, and where I am you cannot come" (cf. 8: 21). But the fate of true disciples is described in a positive way, in the story of the call of the first of them. Jesus asks them: "What are you *looking for?*" (1: 38). And the disciples themselves will answer a little later, declaring: "We have *found* the Messiah" (1: 41) and "we have *found* the one about whom Moses wrote in the law and also the prophets"

---

4. On this theme, see R.-J. Tournay, *Word of God, Song of Love: A Commentary on the Song of Songs*, New York, Paulist, 1988, pp. 72-73 and note 12.

(1:45). Likewise, the two first disciples set about *following* Jesus and, in the end, "*they stayed with him* that day" (1:39). The story of the call of the first disciples is consequently strongly theologized. This invites us to try and find if such a literary process may not also have some sapiential application.

dc) We first read in the book of Wisdom 6:12: "(Wisdom) is readily perceived by those who love her, and found by those who seek her". Likewise the two disciples in John 1:38, 41-45: they have sought and found Jesus. We then read in Wis 6:14: "He who watches for her *at dawn* shall not be disappointed, for he shall find her sitting by his gate". It is the same theme, but with a precision in time. Let us go back then to John 1:41, with the variant we have pointed out above: "He found *in the morning* his own brother Simon and told him, '*We have found* the Messiah'". We therefore have the same temporal note as in Wis 6:14. Finally, in Wis 6:16, the roles are as if reversed: "(Wisdom) makes her own rounds, seeking those worthy of her, and graciously appears to them in the ways". Likewise in John 1:43, Jesus wants to go to Galilee and on his way he meets Philip and invites him to follow him. It is therefore Jesus who, like Wisdom, took the first step. In the story of the call of the first disciples it would thus be Jesus/Wisdom that Andrew and his companion "find", then he takes the initiative of revealing himself to Philip.

4. *Jesus/Wisdom, the Bread Which Gives Life*

The Jews ask Jesus to give them a "sign" like the one done by Moses in the desert when he fed the Hebrews on manna, considered as "bread from heaven" (John 6:31). Jesus answers that it was not Moses that gave the bread from heaven, but the Father (6:32). Besides, the Hebrews ate this bread and they died (6:49) while the true bread given by God is such that if anyone eat of it, he will not die (6:50). What is then this "true" and marvellous bread which enables men to escape from death? Jesus himself is going to explain it.

a) At verse 35 Jesus declares: "I am the bread of life; whoever comes to me will never hunger, and whoever believes in me will never thirst". The sapiential perspective is certain and recognized by all commentators. In Sir 24:19-21 Wisdom invites men in these terms: "Come to me all you that yearn for me... those who eat of me will still be hungry, and those who drink of me will be thirsty". The analogy between the two texts is obvious and the contradiction they offer is only an apparent one. In Sir 24: 21, those who eat of Wisdom will still be hungry in the sense that, once they have tasted it they can no longer do without it. In John 6: 35, Jesus is such perfect nourishment that it satisfies forever. Another sapiential text throws a light on Jesus' assertion. In Prov 9: 5 Wisdom invites men in these terms: "Come, eat of my bread and drink of the wine I have mixed". Bread and wine symbolize the teaching given by Wisdom, as is said clearly in Sir 15: 3: "She (Wisdom) feeds him with the bread of understanding, she gives him to drink the water of wisdom".

Jesus is thus the true bread since he is Wisdom sent to men by God to teach them how to live so as to be pleasing to him (cf. Sir 24: 8; Wis 9: 10).

b) But in what sense does this bread give life and enable men not to die? To understand this we have to go back to the narrative of the fall of the first human couple as told in the first chapters of Genesis. In the garden of Eden were two trees, the tree of life and the tree of the knowledge of good and evil (Gen 2: 9). Adam and Eve could eat of the tree of life, and this secured them an immortality which was not theirs by nature. But God had forbidden them to eat from the tree of the knowledge of good and evil, under pain of death (Gen 2: 17). For having eaten of the fruit of that tree Adam and Eve were chased out of the earthly paradise and, no longer having access to the tree of life, they were condemned to die (Gen 3: 22-24).

Jewish tradition understood that this death sentence was not without a remedy. One can read, for instance, in the Neofiti targum to Gen 3: 24[5]: "For the Law is a tree of life for whoever studies it, and he who keeps its rules lives and continues to exist like the tree of life in the world to come. The Law, for those who keep it in this world, is good like the fruit of the tree of life". Thus the Law is an antidote given to men by God to annihilate the effects of the original curse. If they keep the prescriptions of the Law they will receive

---

5. Translation in A. Diez Macho, *Neophyti 1. Targum Palestinense. Ms de la Biblioteca Vaticana, Tomo I: Genesis*, 1968.

eternal life in the world to come. Though in a less elaborate way this idea could also be found in Prov 3:13, 18 in connection with Wisdom: "Happy is the man who finds wisdom, the man who gains understanding... She is a tree of life to them that lay hold of her and happy is everyone who holds her fast" (cf. Prov 11:30; 13:12; 15:4).

So too for John: Jesus/Wisdom is the "bread of life" inasmuch as he enables us to escape from the original curse. let us compare John 6:51 with Gen 3:22, to which it is contrary:

Gen 3:22   μήποτε... λάβῃ τοῦ ξύλου τῆς ζωῆς καὶ φάγῃ καὶ ζήσεται
             εἰς τὸν αἰῶνα
John 6:51a   ἐάν τις φάγῃ ἐκ τούτου τοῦ ἄρτου ζήσει εἰς τὸν αἰῶνα

Gen 3:22   "lest he... take of the tree of life and eat and live forever"
John 6:51a   "if any man eat of this bread he shall live forever"

Note that the formula "he shall live forever" is only to be found here in the whole Bible (6:58 echoes 6:51). Adam and Eve are excluded from the earthly paradise lest they might eat of the tree of life and live forever. Jesus is the true bread, and if anyone eats of that bread he will live forever. The Johannine phrase "bread of life" (6:35, 48) which is unique in the whole Bible, is probably a transposition of the phrase in Genesis, "tree of life".

We can press further the comparison between the Johannine narrative and that of Genesis. In John 6:37, Jesus declares: "Everything that the Father gives me will come to me, and I will not reject anyone who comes to me (οὐ μὴ ἐκβάλω ἔξω)". Here again we have an opposition with what is said in Genesis 3:24: God "drove out" (ἐξέβαλεν) Adam and made him dwell outside paradise. Anyone that comes to Jesus/Wisdom will not be thrown out of paradise, as if he no longer had access to the tree of life.

In the earthly paradise there were two trees, the tree of the knowledge of good and evil and the tree of life. Adam and Eve could approach the tree of life but they were forbidden to eat of the tree of knowledge. For having transgressed this prohibition, they no longer had access to the tree of life and were doomed to die. But now all has changed. Jesus/Wisdom brings to all the real knowledge of good and evil (cf. Wis 10:8) and they *must* feed upon it as upon some wonderful bread. If they do so they will live forever, being thus freed from the primeval curse.

5. *The Victory over Death*

In 6: 50 Jesus says: "This is the bread that comes from heaven so that one may eat it and not die". This wonderful bread, we have seen, is none other than Jesus/Wisdom (6: 35). In the same line of thought, Jesus could again say to the Jews: "Whoever keeps my word will never see death... he will never taste death" (8: 51-52). Yet, what has changed since Jesus uttered those words? Do not humans die as they did before the coming of Christ? How are we then to understand these mysterious words?

a) In the Bible, our victory over death is considered in two different ways, corresponding to two distinct anthropologies.

aa) This victory was first expressed in terms of "resurrection". Before being put to death by order of Antiochus Epiphanes the second brother in 2 Mac 7 says to the tyrant: "You accursed fiend, you are depriving us of this present life, but the King of the world will raise us up to live again forever. It is for his laws that we are dying" (2 Macc 7: 9; cf. 7: 14-23). But a slightly earlier text calls for special attention, Daniel 12: 2:

ורבים מישני אדמת עפר יקיצו
אלה לחיי עולם ואלה לחרפות לדראון עולם

"Many of those who sleep in the dust of the earth shall awake"

The next part of the verse is difficult. How are we to understand ואלה ... אלה in the Hebrew text? It is often translated by: "*Some* shall live forever, *others* shall be an everlasting horror...". This is what the translator of the Septuagint understood. He renders the Hebrew words by οἱ μέν... οἱ δέ. So too, John 5: 28-29 seems to refer to this text understood as it is in the Septuagint. According to this interpretation Daniel would have considered the resurrection not of all the dead but only of "many" among them. Why such a distinction? Is it because the righteous would rise from the dead and not the wicked? No, as some will rise to eternal life while the others will rise to eternal horror. Cardinal Bernard Alfrink[6] saw the difficulty clearly and he suggested the following answer to solve it. The

---

6. B.J. Alfrink, "L'idée de résurrection d'après Dan. xii, 1.2", *Biblica* 40 (1959) 355-371. The interpretation of Dan 12:2 which he gives has been adopted by many commentators. See one of the more recent: André Lacocque, *The Book of Daniel* (Atlanta: John Knox, 1979) on this verse: "Cardinal Alfrink is convincing when he sees in the double 'elleh' two distinct groups in our text, as in 2 Samuel 2: 13 for example".

passage in Daniel must be put back into its context: that of the great
trial that is about to fall upon the people of God. In the time of the
End, the king of the North will sweep over the country and slay part
of its inhabitants (11:40-45). But, thanks to Michael (the archangel)
"everyone who is found written in the book (of life)" will escape
from death. At this time of the End, there will thus take place a first
separation between men: some will be slain by the invader while
others, all those who are written in the book of life, will be saved
from death. Then will come the moment when "*many* of those who
sleep in the dust of the earth shall awake...". There will therefore be
a new separation, concerning this time those who died before the
great invasion: some, many, will rise, while others will not. Daniel
12:2b takes this double separation into account. This half verse is
made up of two nominal clauses which should be translated, as in
Theodotion:

> οὗτοι εἰς ζωὴν αἰώνιον
> καὶ οὗτοι εἰς ὀνειδισμὸν καὶ εἰς αἰσχύνην αἰώνιον
>
> These (are) for everlasting life
> and those (are) for shame and eternal horror [7]

By "these" we should understand, on the one hand those who,
written in the book of life, have been saved from the slaughter
caused by the invader of the time of the end (12:1c); on the other
hand the great number of those who are going to rise (12:2a). They
form the group of the righteous who are called to everlasting life. By
"those" we must understand: on the one hand those who are
slaughtered by the invader because they were not written in the book
of life, and, on the other hand those who will not rise from the dead.
They are the group of the ungodly doomed to eternal horror (cf. Isa
66:24). Thus Daniel only envisages a resurrection for the righteous,
and all the righteous are to rise from the dead. His text no longer
offers any difficulty.

But a new problem arises: how are we to conceive this resurrection? If we want to understand it, we have to take into account
Semitic anthropology. The ancient Semites, like all early peoples, did
not differentiate the soul from the body. They could only think of
man in his psychosomatic unity. All his psychic life, intelligence,
will, feelings, were conceived (imagined) as emanating from his

---

7. The double demonstrative of the Theodotionic text is found in the Septuagint at
2 Sam 2:13.

physical being, and more precisely from his heart or loins. His heart was the seat of his conscious, intellectual and affective activity (cf. Gen 8:21), whereas his loins were the seat of his passions (Job 19:27; Ps 16:7; 73:21). When, at death, this physical being disappeared, man would lose all his intellectual or sensitive faculties. He was now only a *lifeless* shadow in Sheol, he no longer had any personality. Resurrection was thus conceived not only as a reconstitution by God of the physical being of man to whom he finally gave back the breath of life (cf. Ezek 37:1-14), but also as a return to conscious life, made possible by the coming back to life of his heart and loins. But on this view of resurrection, there must be, between death and resurrection, an indeterminate period during which man practically no longer exists.

ab) Alongside this way of conceiving our victory over death, there is another one which appears in the book of Wisdom and which is strongly influenced by Platonism. The author of the book of Wisdom has, at least in the nine first chapters, adopted a firmly Platonistic anthropology. This can be seen in Wis 9:15, inspired by Plato's *Phaedo* (81c):

Wis: φθαρτὸν γὰρ σῶμα βαρύνει ψυχήν,
       καὶ βρίθει τὸ γεῶδες σκῆνος νοῦν πολυφρόντιδα
Phed: ἐμβριθὲς δέ γε... τοῦτο οἴεσθαι χρὴ εἶναι καὶ βαρὺ καὶ γεῶδες καὶ
       ὁρατόν. Ὁ δὴ καὶ ἔχουσα ἡ τοιαύτη ψυχὴ βαρύνεταί τε καὶ ἕλκε-
       ται πάλιν εἰς τὸν ὁρατὸν τόπον...

Wis: the corruptible body burdens the soul
       and the earthen shelter weighs down the mind that has many
       concerns
Phed: but we must think that this (the body) is heavy and weighty and
       earthy and visible. And as such a soul has it (the body), it is
       weighed down and attracted once more to the visible place...

The author of the book of Wisdom therefore admits that there is a distinction between body and soul[8]. As in Platonic philosophy, he sees death as a separation of the soul from the body. While the visible body dissolves in the earth, the invisible soul can go and join God. In a certain way, what we call death is nothing more than an appearance, since man goes on living through his soul. "The souls of the righteous are in God's hand and no suffering shall touch them. In the eyes of the foolish *they seemed to die*, their passing away was

8. On the Platonic influences on the editing of this text, see C. Larcher, *Le livre de la Sagesse ou la Sagesse de Salomon* (Études Bibliques, n.s., 3), 1984, pp. 595ff.

considered an affliction and their journey away from us as an annihilation, but they are in peace. If, in the eyes of men, they have been chastised, yet is their hope full of *immortality*" (Wis 3: 1-4; cf. 1: 13-15; 2: 23-24). The body may die, but the soul does not; it is immortal. In this sense, the fate of the righteous man who dies may be compared to that of Enoch, the patriarch, of whom the Bible says that because he had been "pleasing to God" God had "transferred" him from earth to heaven (Gen 5: 24, LXX), without his having tasted death, as the rabbinic tradition will say. These same phrases will be taken up again in Wis 4: 10, speaking of the righteous man who dies prematurely: "become 'pleasing to God' he was loved, and, as he lived among sinners, he was 'transferred'".

The author of the book of Wisdom seems however to have cut away from strict Platonism on one important point. For Plato, the human soul was immortal by nature. Such an idea was difficult to assimilate to a biblical perspective. God, indeed, is the author of life. Would not admitting that the soul is immortal deprive God of one of his prerogatives? In Wis 2: 2-3, the ungodly thus describe the final destiny of man according to their own ideas: "We were born through chance, and hereafter we shall be as if we had not existed. The breath of our nostrils is but smoke and thought a spark which spurts out at the beating of our hearts; when it goes out, our body will turn to ashes and our spirit will dissolve like unresisting air". Therefore, according to the godless, there remains nothing of man after his death, he goes back to nothingness. Now it seems as if the author of the book of Wisdom thinks that the impious will suffer precisely the fate they consider as unavoidable; they have made a covenant with death and they belong to it (Wis 1: 16; 2: 24). So immortality is a gift of God which he keeps for the righteous only. The impious are doomed to total destruction.

b) What now about Johannine thought? According to certain passages, John would have adopted the ideas expressed in the book of Daniel: man is to rise at the end of time (6: 39, 40, 44, 54; 12: 48; cf. 5: 27-29 which takes up Daniel 12: 2). But, with Bultmann, we think that these texts were added by the final redactor of the gospel. This is corroborated by an analysis of the dialogue between Jesus and Martha in 11: 23-27. Jesus declares to Martha: "Your brother will rise" (v. 23). We have here, as often in the Fourth Gospel, a word which can be taken in two different senses. Martha understands it according to Daniel: "I know he will rise, in the resurrection on the last day" (v. 24). But Jesus states his thought more precisely in a text which has obviously been overloaded. Let us read it by comparing it for instance to 8:12:

11:25-26	8:12
ἐγώ εἰμι ἡ ἀνάστασις	ἐγώ εἰμι τὸ φῶς τοῦ κόσμου
καὶ ἡ ζωή	
ὁ πιστεύων εἰς ἐμὲ	ὁ ἀκολουθῶν ἐμοὶ
[κἂν ἀποθάνῃ ζήσεται	
καὶ πᾶς ὁ ζῶν	
καί πιστεύων εἰς ἐμὲ]	
οὐ μὴ ἀποθάνῃ εἰς τὸν αἰῶνα	οὐ μὴ περιπατήσῃ ἐν τῇ σκοτίᾳ
	ἀλλ᾽ ἕξει τὸ φῶς τῆς ζωῆς
I am the resurrection and the life,	I am the light of the world.
whoever believes in me,	Whoever follows me
[even if he dies, yet	
shall he live and	
everyone who lives and	
believes in me]	
will never die.	will not walk in darkness,
	but will have the light of
	life.

The added part becomes perceptible, both by the parallel with 8:12, and by the "resumption" constituted by the sequence "whoever believes in me" / "and believes in me". The Johannine final redactor wanted to take into account the fact that, in appearance, all men must die[9].

According to this text Jesus rejects the idea of resurrection as it was conceived by Daniel. He himself is the resurrection. Whoever believes in him will never die, "he has passed from death to life" (5:24). The author of the fourth gospel has therefore adopted an individual eschatology of Platonic inspiration. Through his soul, he who believes in Jesus does not die, in this sense that his soul goes on living; it has acquired immortality. Thus, thanks to Jesus/Wisdom, man can escape the curse weighing on the first human couple; he will never see death since his soul goes on living. His death was but an appearance (cf. Wis 3:2); in fact he has passed from this world to the world above (cf. John 8:23).

---

9. By adding the phrase "even if he die shall live", the final redactor is probably thinking of the resurrection, granted his concern to reintroduce this theme in the passages cited above.

But all of this only makes sense if the author of the Fourth Gospel admits, with the author of the book of Wisdom, that the wicked will not escape from absolute death: they will sink back into the nothingness out of which they had been drawn (cf. Wis 2:2-3)[10].

10. This way of imagining the final destiny of those who refuse to believe in Jesus is only valid if one admits that the soul is not immortal by nature. In the contrary case, one would have to imagine another way to present the punishment of those whom the Bible calls the ungodly.

CHAPTER THREE

THE WORD OF GOD MADE FLESH

Like all the OT prophets, Moses spoke in the name of God. To use the expressions of the book of Exodus, God put his own words in Moses' mouth (Exod 4:15); or again, Moses was the mouth of God (Jer 15:19). But Jesus, surpassing Moses in this, is "the Prophet" par excellence because he is the Word of God made flesh: "And the Word became flesh and dwelt among us" (John 1:14). This theme is developed in the Prologue of the gospel and will be the object of our present inquiry.

Almost all modern authors admit that, to write the Prologue of his gospel (John 1:1-18), John took up and expanded an earlier hymn, probably pre-Christian. But there remains a great variety of choices when it comes to assign what belongs to the earlier hymn and what belongs to the evangelist's expansions[1]. Without going into this problem thoroughly, we will take our start from the results which we have already set out in the third volume of our Synopsis which is devoted to the gospel of John[2].

I. The Original Hymn

The early hymn consisted solely of vv. 1ab, 3-5[3]; it was a hymn to the creator Logos (Word), developed in a wisdom perspective.

1. *Structure of the Original Hymn*

a) When it comes to reconstructing the early hymn, all authors start from the first five verses of the Prologue. But many think, with

---

1. On this problem, see Gerard Rochais, "La formation du Prologue (Jn 1,1-18)", in *Science et Esprit* 37 (1985) 7-9. He sets out quite clearly the positions of 37 authors from 1922 to 1983, indicating only the verses which they keep as composing the early hymn.

2. Boismard-Lamouille, *Synopse* III, pp. 71-79.

3. This is the position we adopted in our John commentary of 1977; it has also been held, and presented as a "new view", by E.L. Miller, "The Logic of the Logos Hymn: A New View", *NTS* 29 (1983) 552-561. G. Rochais holds a similar view, but he retains v. 1c and v. 11.

reason, that the last stich of v. 1 and v. 2 should be excluded[4]. It is clear in the first place that v. 2 does not have the rhythm of vv. 1 and 3-5, as we will point out later. Besides, it only picks up the ideas of v. 1b without carrying the thought further. We are dealing with a "reprise" of a classic type intended to make easier the insertion of the last phrase of v. 1 "and the Logos was God". This sentence fits the Christology of the evangelist, as we will show later on, and it is difficult to attribute it to the early hymn, especially if the hymn was pre-Christian.

b) The early hymn was formed then of eight sentences grouped two by two, each consisting of three elements: a subject, a verb and a complement (or an attribute of the subject). It must have run something like this:

1   ἐν ἀρχῇ · ἦν · ὁ λόγος
    καὶ ὁ λόγος · ἦν · πρὸς τὸν θεόν.
3   πάντα · δι' αὐτοῦ · ἐγένετο
    καὶ χωρὶς αὐτοῦ · ἐγένετο · οὐδὲ ἕν.
4   ὃ γέγονεν ἐν αὐτῷ · ζωὴ · ἦν
    καὶ ἡ ζωὴ · ἦν · τὸ φῶς τῶν ἀνθρώπων
5   καὶ τὸ φῶς · ἐν τῇ σκοτίᾳ · φαίνει
    καὶ ἡ σκοτία · αὐτὸ · οὐ κατέλαβεν.

1   In the beginning ' was ' the Logos
    and the Logos ' was ' close by God.
3   All things ' came into being ' through Him
    and apart from Him ' nothing ' came to be.
4   Whatever came to be in Him ' was ' life
    and life ' was ' the light of man
5   and life ' shines ' in the darkness
    and the darkness, ' it ', did not overcome it.

2. *Some Points to Discuss*

a) The first point to discuss is the interpretation, in v. 1, of the expression πρὸς τὸν θεόν. In classical Greek, the preposition πρός followed by the accusative indicates movement toward a definite goal, person or thing. We would in that case understand that the Logos was "toward God", which invites us to paraphrase, as does the TOB: "... and the Word was *turned toward* God". But we know that, at the time of the NT, the prepositions πρός and εἰς were often

---

4. Of the 37 authors listed by Rochais, 16 consider v. 2 as an addition. Rochais himself adopts this position. Among these 16 authors, 3 also omit v. 1c.

used without any idea of movement and could have the same sense as παρά and ἐν followed by the dative[5]. We should then translate it "was close by God". One could object that this would be the only such case in the gospel. But if we are in the presence of a pre-Johannine hymn, this objection would clearly not be valid.

Several arguments invite us to make of πρός here followed by the accusative the equivalent of παρά followed by the dative. We saw in the preceding chapter that the Prologue of the gospel had as background a certain number of wisdom texts, especially Prov 8: 22-30. In this text Wisdom praises herself by emphasizing the role she played in the work of creation, at God's side. Note then vv. 23-24 LXX: "Before the world he established me, *in the beginning* (ἐν ἀρχῇ), before he made the earth and before he made the depths...". Then v. 30, which refers to the whole work of creation described in this passage: "I was *at his side* (παρ' αὐτῷ), as the master of the work". The parallel of John 1: 1ab, 3 with this text from Proverbs removes all ambiguity from the interpretation of v. 1: "In the beginning (ἐν ἀρχῇ) was the Logos and the Logos was in God's presence (at his side, πρὸς αὐτόν = παρ' αὐτῷ). Through him all things come into being...". Even though the literary parallel be less strict, refer also to Wis 9: 9: "Now with you (μετὰ σοῦ) is Wisdom, who knows your works and was present (παροῦσα) when you made the world". We find the same theme again in John 17: 5, where it is Christ as Wisdom who speaks in allusion to the work of creation: "Do you now, Father, give me glory at your side (παρὰ σοί), a glory I had with you before the world began"[6].

b) Another point of discussion concerns the punctuation between vv. 3 and 4: should the break be placed before or after the expression "whatever came to be" (ὃ γέγονεν)? The solution which we have adopted is based on the following observations. First of all, if we attach the expression in question to v. 3, the second part of this verse is overloaded in relation to the whole. But especially, at v. 4,

---

5. See in this sense F. Blass-A. Debrunner, *Grammatik des neutestamentlichen Griechisch*, § 239, 1-2; F.M. Abel, *Grammaire du grec biblique*, § 50m; M. Zerwick, *Graecitas Biblica exemplis illustratur*, n. 74. These authors cite precisely John 1: 1 as an illustration of this case.

6. In 1 John 1: 2 it is likewise said that eternal life "was with the Father" (ἦν πρὸς τὸν πατέρα) before being manifested. Compare Col 3: 3-4. There is no reason to understand that this eternal life "was turned toward the Father".

we are forced to make the noun "life" the subject of the sentence, but this is impossible since this noun has no article: ζωή. This anomaly is even less tolerable because, in the following stich, the same noun is preceded by the article. In v. 4a, the word "life" can only be attributive, and that requires us to include the expression "whatever came to be" in this v. 4a, as subject of the sentence.

Moreover, in the gospel of John, a noun in the attributive position loses its article, even if it is determinate, when it is placed in front of the verb of the sentence. This rule is well illustrated in John 1:49, in Nathanael's confession of faith: "Rabbi, you are the son of God, you (the) king of Israel". In the first sentence, the attribute is placed *after* the verb and thus has an article: σὺ εἶ ὁ υἱὸς τοῦ θεοῦ. But in the second, it is placed *before* the verb and so loses its article: σὺ βασιλεὺς εἶ τοῦ 'Ισραήλ. In John 1:4a, even though it has no article, the word "life" is placed *before* the verb; grammatically speaking, it could therefore be either determinate or indeterminate. We think that it is determinate since it will be so in v. 4b.

Finally, how should we translate the expression ἐν αὐτῷ? In classical Greek, this would be "in him". But, under the influence of Hebrew, this Greek preposition often acquires the instrumental sense, as if there were δι' αὐτοῦ. This sense seems best here due to the influence of Wis 9:1a-2b: "You who have made all things by your word (ἐν λόγῳ σου)".

c) A last difficulty occurs in the last sentence of the hymn, at the end of v. 5: καὶ ἡ σκοτία αὐτὸ οὐ κατέλαβεν. What is the meaning of the verb? The general idea is to grasp or seize; but there are numerous derived senses: take, overtake, come upon, make one's own, catch, constrain, grasp intellectually, understand. Here again our guide should be texts from the wisdom books; this will link us up with the interpretation given by the majority of the ancient Greek fathers. We read in Wis 7:29-30: "She [Wisdom] is more beautiful than the sun... Compared with the light she is found to be superior, for it is succeeded by the night, but against wisdom evil does not prevail (οὐ κατισχύει)". Similarly, we read in the Odes of Solomon, a Christian work from the end of the first century: "Let not light be conquered by darkness, nor let truth flee from falsehood" (18:6; Charlesworth, *OTP* 2.751). We will have the same idea in the Prologue hymn: the darkness has not been able to overcome (or put out) the light.

3. *A Hymn to the Creator Logos*

The original hymn praised the role which the Logos played in the work of creation, in reference to the creation of the world (Gen 1:1–2:4)[7] and in a wisdom perspective.

a) The creation story, Gen 1:1, opens with these words: "In the beginning, God made the heavens and the earth". The initial expression recurs at the beginning of the Prologue of John's gospel: "In the beginning was the Logos". The borrowing from the Genesis account, recognized by all commentators, is the more certain because the role of the Logos in creation will be affirmed from v. 3: "All things were made through him". Thus, from the beginning of the created world, the Logos "was". He existed even before the world's creation, "with God"; this goes without saying since the world was created through him (v. 3). This takes up the idea expressed in connection with Wisdom in Prov 8:22-30: "The Lord created me at the beginning of his ways, the first of his acts of old. Ages ago I was set up, at the first, before the beginning of the earth. When there were no depths I was brought forth, when there were no springs abounding with water... When he established the heavens, I was there... When he marked out the foundations of the earth, then I was beside him, like a master workman".

b) In Gen 1:3, the first stage in the world's creation occurs in this way: "And God said: 'Let there be light'; and there was light (καὶ ἐγένετο φῶς)". It suffices then for God to give an order, a "word", for light to come to exist. It is the Word of God which saw to it that the light "was". The same holds true for all the stages of creation: "And God said: 'Let there be a firmament...', and it was so" (LXX Gen 1:6; cf. 1:9, 11, 14-15, 20-24). Already in Wis 9:1b-2a the work of creation had been summarized in this phrase: "You who have made all things (τὰ πάντα) by our word" (cf. Ps 33:6). The hymn of John's Prologue summarized it in the same way, but giving a better echo of the text of Genesis: πάντα δι᾽ αὐτοῦ ἐγένετο, "All things were made through him", all things were made by the Logos of God, who "was beside God" "in the beginning", when God undertook the work of creation.

7. We take up here, and add a bit to, the ideas set forth by Peder Borgen, "Observations on the Targumic Character of the Prologue of John", *NTS* 16 (1969/70) 288-295.

c) On the first day, God created the light, "and he separated the light from the darkness" (Gen 1:3-4). On the sixth day, which was also the last, God created living creatures: "And God said: 'Let the earth bring forth every living creature (ψυχὴν ζῶσαν — נפש חיה) according to their kinds...'. And it was so" (1:24). That same day, to finish his work, God created mankind: "And God said: 'Let us make man in our image, after our likeness...'. So God created man in his own image, in the image of God he created him; male and female he created them..." (1:26-27). The light which was set over against the darkness from the first day on; life and man created on the last day... These are realities which reappear in vv. 4-5 of John's Prologue: "In him was life, and the life was the light of men. The light shines in the darkness, and the darkness has not overcome it". The hymn takes up the work of creation in inverse order, ending with the opposition between light and darkness.

The hymn taken up by the evangelist at the beginning of the Prologue of his gospel is indeed to the glory of the creator Logos, a free imitation of Gen 1:1–2:4 in a wisdom perspective.

II. The Work of the Evangelist

Let us now see how the evangelist has taken up this hymn, completing it in such a way as to introduce his own ideas.

A. *The Logos and New Creation*

As he took up the original hymn, the evangelist added to it vv. 6 to 18. But he did so from a very precise viewpoint; he wanted to show that, when the Logos became flesh, he had his role to play, not only in the work of creation, but also in the re-creation of humanity.

1. *The Structure of the Prologue*

The Prologue of John's gospel offers a certain number of elements which correspond two by two, in an inverse order. Vv. 1 and 2 speak of the relations between the Logos and God: he was "beside God"; this expression, used in v. 1, is repeated in v. 2. In the same way, v. 18 speaks of the relations between the Only-Begotten and the

Father: he is "in the bosom of the Father". — V. 3 highlights the role of the Logos in creation: "All things were made through him"[8]. V. 17 indicates Jesus' role in the new economy of salvation: "Grace and truth (or: goodness and fidelity) came through Jesus Christ". — The parallelism between vv. 4-5 and 16 is less apparent, but just as real. In vv. 4-5, we have the description of the benefits which flow from the creative work of the Logos: life and light for humans. In v. 16, we learn that from the fullness of the Only-Begotten, we have all received. — In vv. 6-8 and 15, the parallelism becomes again very clear: it is a matter of John the Baptist's witness. — Vv. 9-11 describe how the Logos came into the world, then to his own. This coming of the Logos is again affirmed in v. 14: "And the Word became flesh and he dwelt among us...". Only vv. 12-13 have no parallel: they form the center of the Prologue.

We see then that the structure of the Prologue consists in a quite classical chiasm:

A	1-2	The Logos with God
B	3	The role of the Logos in creation
C	4-5	The benefits which he has brought to humanity
D	6-8	John the Baptist bears witness
E	9-11	The Logos comes into the world, to his own
F	12-13	He gave us to become children of God
E¹	14	The Logos made flesh has come among us the Only-Begotten
D¹	15	John the Baptist bears witness
C¹	16	We receive of his fulness
B¹	17	The role of the Only-Begotten in re-creation
A¹	18	The Only-Begotten in the bosom of the Father

The chiastic structure implies a double movement, descending and ascending[9]. We start from God (A) and we find ourselves again in God (A¹) after having descended to the world (9-14): This is the double movement which the Christ expresses in John 16:28: "I come from the Father and have come into the world; again, I am leaving the world and going to the Father". But let us not forget

---

8. V. 10 also contains the phrase "and the world was made through him", but this recalling of v. 3 does not give the essential idea of the verse. Its point is to stress how the world is without excuse for not having known/recognized/acknowledged the Logos. We could gloss it: "Although the world had been created through him, the world knew him not".

9. In taking up this chiastic structure, Culpepper proposes to make it more precise at vv. 12-13; vv. 12a and 13 would be in parallel, and v. 12b would form the pivot of the Prologue. Cf. R.A. Culpepper, "The Pivot of John's Prologue", *NTS* 27 (1981) 1-31.

that it is the Logos, the Word, who accomplishes this double movement. How then can we not think of this great text from the prophet Isaiah:

> For as the rain and the snow come down from heaven, and return not thither but water the earth, making it bring forth and sprout, giving seed to the sower and bread to the eater, so shall my word be that goes forth from my mouth; it shall not return to me empty, but it shall accomplish that which I propose (Isa 55: 10-11).

Not only is the double movement of the Word identical in Isa 55: 10-11 and in the Prologue of John's gospel, but the result of the sending out by God is analogous: the rain renders the earth fertile and makes it bear fruit and gives seed to the sower; so too the Logos gives to those who receive him power to become "children of God" (John 1: 12-13)[10].

2. *The New Birth*

We find here a classic theme of the New Testament, a new birth worked in us thanks to the Word of God. This theme already appears in the parable of the sower, or better, in the interpretation of this parable. "The sower sows the Word" runs Mark 4: 14; and Luke 8: 11, more clearly "The seed is the Word of God". We must "receive" this Word (Luke 8: 13) and keep it in our heart, symbolized by the good earth, for it to bear fruit (8: 15). The Word is thus in the heart of man as the seed which the sower throws onto the good soil; it will produce more or less abundant grain; thirtyfold, sixtyfold, a hundredfold for one seed. The reader can easily understand that these grains represent the good works inspired in each person by the Word which he has received in his heart.

The letters of James, Peter and John will take up this theme while enriching it with a harmonics: the theme of the new birth[11].

> Do not be deceived, my beloved brethren. Every good endowment and every perfect gift *is from above, coming from the Father of lights* with whom there is no variation or shadow due to change. Of his own will *he brought us forth by the word* of truth that we should be a kind of first fruits of his creatures... Therefore put away all filthiness and rank growth of

---

10. This parallelism with Isaiah shows that it is indeed vv. 12-13 which form the center of the Prologue, and not v. 14 as many commentators think.

11. Cf. M.-É. Boismard, "Une liturgie baptismale dans la *Prima Petri*", *RB* 63 (1956) 182-208 and 64 (1957) 161-183; reprinted in *Moïse ou Jésus*, pp. 159-216 (Appendix II).

wickedness and *receive with meekness the implanted word*, which is able to save your souls. But *be doers of the word*, and not hearers only... (Jas 1:16-22).

Having purified your souls by your obedience to the truth for a sincere love of the brethren, love one another earnestly from the heart. *You have been born anew, not of perishable seed but of imperishable, through the living and abiding word of God*; for "All flesh is like grass and all its glory like the flower of grass. The grass withers, and the flower falls, but the word of the Lord abides forever"... So put away all malice... (1 Peter 1:22–2:1; Isa 40:6-8).

See what love the Father has given us, that we should be called *children of God*; and so we are... No one *born of God* commits sin; for God's nature [seed] abides in him, and he cannot sin because he is *born of God*. By this it may be seen who are *the children of God*, and who are the children of the devil: whoever does not do right is not of God, nor he who does not love his brother (1 John 3:1, 9-10).

I write to you, young men, because you are strong, and *the word of God* abides in you, and you have overcome the evil one (1 John 2:14; cf. 1:1).

All these texts develop the same theme: the disciple of Jesus has received in himself the Word of God as a seed of life; this seed is at the beginning of a new birth which expands in love. They rejoin the central theme of the Prologue of John's gospel: all those who have received the Logos, to them has he given power "to become children of God". But the Prologue surpasses all the other texts in depth. In the letters of Peter and James, the word which we receive is the gospel preaching, as 1 Peter 1:25 says explicitly. In the Prologue, the Word is a person, who was with God, who was God, who took flesh to come dwell among us.

B. *Jesus Christ and Moses*

We read in v. 17 of the Prologue: "The law was given through Moses, goodness and faithfulness[12] came (ἐγένετο) *through Jesus Christ*". This text gives an antithetical parallelism between Moses and Jesus which we must explain now. But the expression "goodness and faithfulness" occurs already in v. 14, and v. 17 cannot be understood without v. 14. In fact it is the entire block vv. 14-18 whose meaning

---

12. Usually these words are translated "grace and truth" (cf. RSV and revised NAB), but the word "grace" leads to confusion, and it is a matter of "faithfulness" and certainly not "truth". We will justify further on the translation we give here.

must be deepened if one wants to understand the antithetical
parallelism of v. 17 between Moses and Jesus.

John 1: 14-18 and Exod 33-34[13]

Before comparing the Johannine texts with those from Exodus, let
us rapidly see what the sequence of the episodes recounted in Exod
33-34 is. God had concluded with the Hebrews a covenant sealed by
the gift of the Law (Exod 19-20). But the Hebrews broke the
covenant, giving themselves up to idolatry at the episode of the
Golden Calf, and this led Moses to break the tables of the Law
(Exod 32). God rejected the unfaithful people. He then orders them
to continue on their way to the promised Land; but he will not go
up with them because of their unfaithfulness (33: 1-3). Moses insists
that God go back on his decision; his presence is indispensable to
protect the Hebrews against their enemies whom they will meet
along their way (33: 15-16). God agrees, but Moses wants a visible
proof of this presence; he asks to see God (33: 17-18). But God
answers him that it is not possible for a man to see God (33: 19-23).
He will nevertheless agree to Moses' request as far as possible;
Moses will not see his face, but "from behind"; and it is in the
course of this theophany that God reveals to Moses his name, that
is, who he is (34: 1-7). Finally, God agrees to leave with the Hebrews
(34: 9), then he dictates the Law a second time to Moses who puts it
down in writing (34: 10-28). Having come down from the mountain,
Moses at times converses with God in the tent of Witness, at times
returns to the Hebrews to tell them everything which God has
commanded them (34: 29-34).

a) One of the themes which underlies this whole account of
Exodus is that of the divine presence (Exod 33: 15-16; 34: 9). Now
v. 14 of the Prologue describes the way in which God makes himself
present now: "And the Logos became flesh and dwelt among us".
Let us not forget that the Logos is God (1: 1); it is therefore God

---

13. In regard to the comparison between these two biblical passages, Rochais (p. 32)
writes: "This idea, proposed from the beginning of the century and well developed by
Boismard in 1953, has since then become well known and, it seems, commonly accepted".
He himself in any case refuses to accept such an exegesis even though he recognizes a
certain number of contacts between the two texts, especially for the expression "full of
grace and truth" (p. 33). But his refusal stems perhaps from his wanting to place on two
different redactional levels vv. 14, 16 on the one hand, 17-18 on the other.

himself who comes to dwell among us by becoming "flesh". This last word should be taken in its traditional biblical sense; man, but insofar as he is corruptible and naturally doomed to death (cf. Gen 6: 3; Isa 40: 6-7).

b) In the Exodus story, God agrees to come with his people, but Moses asks for a proof of his presence: "Show me thy glory" (33: 18). The glory of God was in fact the manifesting of his presence (cf. Exod 24: 15-17). But God refuses: "You cannot see my face; for man shall not see me and live" (Exod 33: 20). He will nonetheless agree up to a point with Moses' request: "Behold, there is a place by me where you will stand upon the rock; and while my glory passes by I will put you in a cleft of the rock, and I will cover you with my hand until I have passed by; then I will take away my hand, and you shall see my back; but my face shall not be seen" (Exod 33: 21-23). What was impossible for Moses has become possible for us thanks to the Logos incarnate. No doubt the principle remains: "No one has ever seen God" (John 1: 18; cf. 6: 46; 1 John 4: 12)[14]; it is impossible for man to see God. But the evangelist says of the incarnate Logos: "And we have seen his glory" (1: 14), glory which he holds from the Father. This glory can then be seen now, but because it is as if veiled by the humanity which the Logos has assumed.

c) God then wants to accompany his people during their peregrinations in the desert. And as the Hebrews then lived in tents, Moses, at God's order, has a tent built which will be as it were the dwelling of God during the Exodus (Exod 36: 8-19). When all the works are finished, God will take possession of them: "The cloud covered the Tent of Meeting and the glory of Yahweh filled the Tabernacle. And Moses was not able to enter the Tent of Meeting, because the cloud abode upon it, and the glory of the Lord filled the Tabernacle" (Exod 40: 34-35). Let us now reread John 1: 14: "And the Logos became flesh and dwelt among us, and we have seen his glory...". To say "dwelt", the evangelist uses the verb ἐσκήνωσεν, derived from σκηνή which means "tent". One could thus translate it: "he pitched his tent among us". The humanity which he comes to assume is like the tent under which he dwells with the radiance of his

---

14. John 1: 18 is also probably inspired by Sir 43: 31 where it is said of God: "Who has seen him and can describe him?" (τίς ἑόρακεν αὐτὸν καὶ ἐκδιηγήσεται).

glory. He dwells among us thus as Yahweh dwelt in the midst of his people during the Exodus.

d) God has then restored his covenant with his people and, consequently, he gives Moses the order to write anew his commandments on the tables of the covenant, which Moses does while he dwells with God for forty days and forty nights (Exod 34: 27-28). This event is reported in John 1: 17: "The law was given through Moses...".

e) But after all, why did God forgive his unfaithfull people? Why did he go back on his decision to leave the Hebrews to their sorry fate? The answer is given in the Name which God gives himself in passing near Moses hidden in the cleft of the rock. God had promised Moses to proclaim his Name before him (Exod 33: 19), that is, to reveal to him who he was. He does it during the theophany narrated in Exod 34: 6. While passing near Moses, he proclaims that he is "a God merciful and gracious, slow to anger, and *abounding in steadfast love and faithfulness*". The last phrase reads in Hebrew רב חסד ואמת; we think that this is found again in the phrase πλήρης χάριτος καὶ ἀληθείας which, in John 1: 14, characterizes the incarnate Logos, or the Only-Begotten.

The equivalence between אמת and ἀλήθεια is obvious, but the meaning is rather that of "faithfulness" than of "truth". Although the word חסד is usually translated by the Septuagint as ἔλεος, its Greek equivalent is rather χάρις, as J.A. Montgomery has well shown[15]. The two nouns of the Hebrew text are then well represented by the two nouns of John's text. There remains the equivalence between רב and πλήρης; this is less obvious, but nevertheless real. The Hebrew adjective means "numerous, great, powerful", but with important nuances. The translation "abounding in, full of" is often demanded by the sense of the passage. This is precisely what is adopted by recent French translations of the Bible (TOB and BJ) in Exod 34: 6; they translate by "riche en bonté et en fidélité" (BJ), or "plein de fidélité et de loyauté" (TOB)[16]. Ps 86: 15 takes up the same phrase and the BJ translates by "plein d'amour et de vérité"

---

15. J.A. Montgomery, "Hebrew Hesed and Greek Charis", *HTR* 32 (1939) 97-102.
16. The translation of the two nouns, especially in the order in which they are given, is unsatisfactory!

(full of love and truth). Why could the evangelist not have had the same reaction when translating the Hebrew text of Exod 34:6?

What is the exact meaning of this formula? The word חסד covers a rather complex notion[17]. It is goodness, kindness, goodwill, favor, but implying a certain moral obligation. In the Exodus story, God was bound to show himself good toward his people on account of the covenant made with them. אמת is faithfulness to this kindness, in spite of everything. The Hebrews rebelled against God when they broke the covenant in the episode of the Golden Calf. But God is the "God merciful and gracious, slow to anger, abounding in steadfast love and faithfulness, keeping steadfast love for thousands..." (Exod 34:6-7). Because he is faithful, while the Hebrews showed themselves unfaithful, God, in his love, agrees to renew the covenant, to act as though nothing had happened. This idea is well expressed in Neh 9:16-19 which takes up the text of Exodus. After having recalled all the kindness of God to his people, the text continues: "But they and our fathers acted presumptuously and stiffened their neck and did not obey your commandments; they refused to obey... But you are a God ready to forgive, gracious and merciful, slow to anger and abounding in steadfast love (רב חסד): and did not forsake them. Even when they had made for themselves a molten calf and said, 'This is your God who brought you up out of Egypt', and had committed great blasphemies, you in your great mercies did not forsake them in the wilderness...". The faithfulness of God is inseparable from his will to forgive the faults and the rebels: "Who is a God like you, pardoning iniquity and passing over transgression for the remnant of his inheritance? He does not retain his anger forever because he delights in steadfast love (חסד). He will again have compassion upon us, he will tread our iniquities under foot. You will cast all our sins into the depths of the sea. You will show faithfulness (אמת) to Jacob and steadfast love (חסד) to Abraham, as you have sworn to our fathers from the days of old" (Mich 7:18-20)[18].

17. H.J. Stoebe has given a good analysis of this word in *TDOT*, ed. E. Jenni and C. Westermann (1971), col. 600-621. — See also K.D. Sakenfeld, *The Meaning of Hesed in the Hebrew Bible* (HSM 17), 1978.

18. The text of Exod 34:6 has had many echoes in the Bible; it is taken up, among others, in Ps 86:5, 15; Ps 103:8; Ps 145:8; Sir 2:11; Joel 2:13.

f) We can now return to the antithetic parallelism of John 1:17: "The law was given by Moses, *kindness and faithfulness* came through Jesus Christ". Jesus Christ *is* the incarnate Logos (1:14). In this sense, he is indeed superior to Moses. Moses only transmitted to men what God spoke to him. Jesus is God himself (1:1) speaking to men. But Jesus *is* also "kindness and faithfulness" incarnate. At the same time as God comes to us to tell us what we should do, how we should act to please him, he also comes to assure us of his unfailing love; even if we revolt against him, even if we refuse to obey him, he is always ready to forgive, to forget our rebellions. Jesus *is* at the same time Law, and Love which forgives rebellions against the Law[19].

---

19. The evangelist accepts without hesitation this idea of the limitless faithfulness of God to his love. In the Hebrew Bible however, we note a certain tendency to minimize the range of the text Exod 34:6-7a. To this text a later hand has added v. 7b: "but who will by no means clear the guilty, visiting the iniquity of the fathers upon the children and the children's children, to the third and the fourth generation". In the same way, Exod 20:5-6 and Deut 5:9-10 first give an equivalent of Exod 34:7b, and only then Exod 34:6-7a.

CHAPTER FOUR

THE ONLY-BEGOTTEN

In the Prologue of the Gospel, Jesus is twice called the "Only-begotten son" (μονογενής)[1]. How should this relationship of Father to Son which unites him to God be understood? In order to avoid possible misunderstandings, we must first analyze the import of the expression "son of God" which the Gospel gives to Jesus. Then we will attempt to understand what John means by "Only-begotten son".

I. JESUS, SON OF GOD

At his initial encounter with Jesus, Nathanael proclaims: "Rabbi, you are the Son of God, you are the King of Israel" (John 1:49). Later, Martha in turn made her profession of faith: "Yes, Lord, I believe that you are the Christ, the Son of God, he who is coming into the world" (11:27). What significance should we give to this double profession of faith? Does it imply recognition by Nathanael, then by Martha, of the divinity of Jesus? It is impossible, however, that Nathanael would have recognized the divinity of Jesus at the time of their first meeting, before Christ had even begun his public life. It is also very unlikely that the evangelist would have attributed such knowledge to him. What then is the exact meaning of the title "son of God"?

1. The Title "Son of God" in the Old Testament

a) In 2 Sam 7:9-16, God orders the prophet Nathan to transmit this message to king David:

> "⁹ I have been with you wherever you went, and have cut off all your enemies from before you; and I will make for you a great name, like the name of the great ones of the earth. ¹⁰ And I will appoint a place for my people Israel, and will plant them, that they may dwell in their own place, and be disturbed no more; and violent men shall afflict them no more, as

---

1. Jn 1:14, 18; cf. 3:16, 18; 1 Jn 4:9.

formerly, [11] from the time that I appointed judges over my people Israel; and I will give you rest from all your enemies. Moreover the Lord declares to you that the Lord will make you a house. [12] When your days are fulfilled and you lie down with your fathers, I will raise up your son after you, who shall come forth from your body, and I will establish his kingdom. [13] He shall build a house for my name, and I will establish the throne of his kingdom for ever. [14] I will be his father, and he shall be my son. When he commits iniquity, I will chasten him with the rod of men, with the stripes of the sons of men; [15] but I will not take my steadfast love from him, as I took it from Saul, whom I put away from before you. [16] And your house and your kingdom shall be made sure for ever before me; your throne shall be established for ever".

This prophecy addressed to David concerns above all his progeny: all his issue who would be called to rule after him. God would establish a special covenant with each of his decendants: "I will be his father and he shall be my son". This is a rite of adoption well known in the ancient East[2]. What exactly does it imply? First of all, it implies God's right to chastise the king who acts wrongly, just as a father chastises his son to correct him (v. 14b). It also implies, however, an effective protection on God's part. This theme underlies the whole of this prophecy. God will be "with him" as he was with David (v. 16), to rid him of his enemies (v. 11). As a result, his royal throne will be solidly established for ever. This promise, expressed just before the declaration of adoption (v. 13), is reiterated at the end of the prophecy in a double form to accentuate its solemnity (v. 16). The "father/son" relationship which unites God to the king descended from David expresses in fact a true covenant: the king must act in accordance with the will of God; in return, God undertakes to protect the king against all enemies, such that his throne survives for ever. These were the very clauses of the covenant between God and his people: the people must faithfully observe the divine Law, and God, for his part, commits himself to protect his people (Exod 19: 3-8; 34: 10-11).

This prophecy of Nathan to David is also reported in analogous terms in 1 Chr 17: 3-14. Note, however, that the author of the book of Chronicles has removed 2 Sam 7: 14b, that is, the clause implying punishment by God of an unfaithful king. The prophecy is thus

---

2. Cf. H. Gressmann, *Der Messias* (FRLANT 43, NF 26), 1929, pp. 29-38. In the Bible, this adoption does not imply a divinisation of the king; on this problem, see R. de Vaux, *Les institutions de l'Ancien Testament*, Paris, 1958-60, vol. I, pp. 171 ff.

entirely centered on the protection that God must provide to him whom he has adopted as his son.

What remained of these divine promises during the Babylonian exile? A psalmist (Ps 89) complains bitterly to God recalling the promises made to David through the prophet Nathan. For him, these promises constitute a true covenant: "I have made a covenant with my chosen one, I have sworn to David my servant: I will establish your line for ever, and build thy throne for all generations" (vv. 3-5; cf. vv. 29, 35, 40). God retains unquestionably the right to punish the king who does not observe his commandments, but without withdrawing his love from him on this account (vv. 31-34). Since God is the father of the king (v. 27), he must *protect him* from all his enemies (vv. 22-26; 28-30; 37-38). This is very much the dominant idea in the prophecy of Nathan to David.

b) It is also the theme developed in the second psalm. The nations and the peoples are in turmoil, the kings of the earth and the princes rebel against God and against him whom he has marked with His royal anointing (vv. 1-2). God, therefore, solemnly declares in his anger: "I have set my king on Zion, my holy hill". The king himself then announces the decree of God:

> [7] He said to me: "You are my son, today I have begotten you. [8] Ask of me, and I will make the nations your heritage, and the ends of the earth your possession. [9] You shall break them with a rod of iron, and dash them in pieces like a potter's vessel.

At the same time he crowned his king in Zion, God proclaimed him his son. He begot him the day he established him as king. As a result, he has empowered him to break all who have rebelled against him in order to establish his kingdom for ever.

c) One can read an analogous theme in Psalm 110 (109) in the Septuagint.

> [1] The Lord said to my Lord, "Sit at my right hand, till I make your enemies your footstool". [2] The Lord sends forth from Zion your mighty scepter, and you will rule in the midst of your foes. [3] The royal dignity is yours in the day of your power, in the splendor of your saints; from the womb, before the dawn, I begot you.

The theme of adoptive sonship of the king, sharing the throne of God, is expressed with as much realism here as in Psalm 2. In both psalms the essential importance is placed on the theme of the victory of the king consecrated by God over his enemies.

d) With the text of Wis 2:16-20, the horizon is broadened. It is no longer a case of the relations between God and the king he has consecrated over his people, but of the just man who observes the divine law. We see him exposed to the hatred of the ungodly, whose manner of life, contemptuous of the laws of God, he criticizes. The ungodly mock him in these terms:

> [16] He takes us for something adulterated and avoids our ways as he would filth. He proclaims the final end of the upright as blessed and *he boasts of having God for his father.* [17] Let us see if what he says is true, and test him to see what sort of end he will have. [18] For *if the just man is the son of God*, He will help him and rescue him from the hands of his enemies. [19] Let us test him with cruelty and with torture, and thus know his gentleness and put his patience to the test. [20] Let us condemn him to a shameful death since, according to what he says, he will be saved.

Even more clearly here than in the royal prophecies we just saw, the title "son of God" implies divine protection. It is proper for God to save the just man from the enemies who seek his life because he is his "father". The ungodly, however, do not understand that even if the just man is put to death, this death is only apparent, because God allows him to continue his life, his true life, the life of his soul with Him. "The souls of the just are in the hands of God, and no torment can touch them. To the unenlightened they appeared to die, their leaving us like a misfortune, but they are at peace" (Wis 3:1-4). All of this is written, obviously, from a more or less Platonist point of view (cf. Wis 9:15, which plagiarizes a passage from the *Phaedo* of Plato). Physical death is only an appearance since the soul goes to God upon leaving the body[3].

Thus in the Old Testament the title "son of God" by no means implies man's participation in divinity, whether he be a king or a just man. It signifies an adoption by God, but not a participation in the divine nature. It is a title which only applies to man as man.

2. *The Title "Son of God" in the Gospel of John*

a) The first time this title is given to Jesus is in the profession of faith of Nathanael: "Rabbi, you are the Son of God, you are the King of Israel" (1:49). As we have already noted, it is impossible

---

3. Contrary to what Plato taught, the author of the book of Wisdom does not hold the soul to be immortal by nature. According to Wis 2:2-3, 23; 1:16, the ungodly will sink into nothingness. Immortality is a gift of God.

that Nathanael would have confessed the divinity of Jesus as early as his first meeting with him, when Jesus had not yet even begun his public life. It would also be unlikely that the evangelist would have had him profess a faith with such sweeping implications. Since this title "son of God" is used in parallel with that of "king of Israel", it only affirms an adoptive relationship, as in the prophecy of Nathan or as in Psalms 2 and 110 (LXX) which imply the protection of God.

b) This is confirmed for us by the passage recounting the appearance of the resurrected Jesus to Mary Magdalen. Once he had allowed her to recognize him, he gives her this message: "Go to my brethren and say to them: 'I am ascending to my Father and your Father, to my God and your God'" (John 20:17). There is a double parallel construction in this phrase of Jesus': between the titles of "Father" and "God" on the one hand, and between Jesus and his brethren, that is his disciples, on the other.

The first parallel is easily explained from the perspective of the Old Testament texts we have previously analyzed. F. Dreyfus demonstrated that the expression "God of" implied God's protection of those who recognized him as their God. There is therefore a certain equivalence between the expressions "God of" and "protector of"[4]. We have seen, however, that in the Old Testament the fatherhood of God toward the king of his people or toward the just man also implied protection on God's part. When Jesus announces that he is ascending to his Father and his God, he is therefore declaring that he is going to rejoin him who just showed his sovereign protection of him in raising him from the dead. It is the answer to the sarcasm of the ungodly as reported in Wisdom 2:18: "If the just man is the son of God, He will help him and rescue him from the hands of his enemies". The same theme can be read in the Synoptics. When Jesus dies on the cross, the Roman centurion proclaims: "Truly, this man was a son of God" (Mark 15:39; Matt 27:54). Luke gives the same meaning to the phrase in altering it slightly: "Truly, this was a just man" (Luke 23:47). For Luke, then, it is the text of Wis 2:18 which is the background of the Roman centurion's profession of faith. This theme is, furthermore, not a new one in the Synoptic Gospels. In the account of the temptation,

---

4. F. DREYFUS, "L'argument scripturaire de Jésus en faveur de la résurrection des morts (Mc xii.26-28)", in *RB* 66 (1959) 213-224.

it is clear that the words of the Tempter of Jesus, reported in Matt 4: 3-6 (cf. Luke 4: 3-9), assume that the quality of "son of God" (cf. Matt 3: 17) implies a special protection on God's part. It will miraculously procure bread for Jesus, or send an angel such that he will not be crushed against the ground.

The theme of the kingship of Jesus, however, is also present in the Johannine text (20: 17). Paraphrasing the prophesy of Nathan to David, as we have seen, Ps 89: 26-27 recalls God's promise to David's royal line in these terms: "You are *my Father, my God* and the Rock of *my salvation*!". Jesus undoubtedly takes up this text when he says, "I am ascending to *my Father...* to *my God...*", to him who has just *saved* him from death. This subtle allusion to the royalty of Jesus, solidly established in spite of the appearances, is linked by implication to Nathanael's profession of faith: "Rabbi, you are the Son God, you are King of Israel" (1: 49).

John 20: 17 also contains a parallel between Jesus and his disciples: "I am ascending to my Father and your Father, to my God and your God". God is not only the Father and God of Jesus, but also the Father and God of the disciples. This confirms for us that God's fatherhood with respect to Jesus extends also to all the disciples and therefore does not have a transcendent meaning. It also indicates, however, that the disciples can hope for the protection of God at the moment of their death: God will return them to life just as he did to Christ.

c) There is no reason to attribute a different meaning to Martha's profession of faith: "Yes, Lord, I believe that you are the Christ, the Son of God, who is coming into the world" (11: 27). The Christ is he who has been anointed as king over the new people of God. This returns to the theme of Ps 2: 1-11. The kings of the earth and princes have allied themselves against God and against his anointed (= Christ). God, however, enthrones him king saying, "You are my son, today I have begotten you". Note that Martha's profession of faith is situated in the context of victory over death, after Jesus affirms, "I am the resurrection and the life" (11: 26).

d) There exist nevertheless two texts which give a transcendent meaning to the title "son of God" attributed to Jesus, and both of them recount accusations made by the Jews against Jesus. They are John 19: 7 and John 10: 33. In the first, the Jews declare to Pilate:

"We have a law, and by that law he ought to die because he has made himself the son of God". In the eyes of the Jews, therefore, the title "son of God" had a transcendent quality, and since Jesus attributed it to himself, he must die because he made himself God's equal.

The second text is the more interesting one, because it gives us the thinking of the evangelist on the meaning of the title "son of God" at the same time that it brings us subtly back to the theme of Jesus as the new Moses[5]. The Jews want to stone Jesus because he has blasphemed: although he is only a man, he has made himself God (10:33). By "he made himself God", one must understand that he called himself "son of God", as Jesus did in the answer he gave them (10:36). "Son of God" is therefore clearly the same as "God". But let us look closer at the answer Jesus gave to this accusation:

> Is it not written in your Law: 'I said, you are gods'? If the Law calls "gods" those to whom the word of God came (and Scripture cannot be broken) do you say of him whom the Father consecrated and sent into the world, 'you are blaspheming', because I said, 'I am the Son of God'?

In his answer to the Jews, Jesus makes an appeal first to Scripture. The term "Law" should be understood in the broad sense, since the text to which Jesus refers is Ps 82:6: "I say, You are gods, sons of the Most High, all of you". We therefore find in this psalm, once again, an equivalence between "god" and "sons of God". The people of whom the psalm speaks are actually the judges charged with rendering justice in Israel. But Jewish tradition[6] put this passage from the psalm in relation with Deut 1:16-17, a text in which Moses, unable to carry alone the burdens and judgments on the people he must lead into the promised land (1:12), has capable men selected from each of the tribes and sets them up as "chiefs" (1:13-15). From then on it is they who have the responsibility to render justice (1:16-17), at least in relatively easy cases. The most difficult cases still fall under the jurisdiction of Moses (1:17). According to Deut 1:9-18 then, Moses was originally the "only" judge in Israel. In order to lighten an otherwise too heavy load, part

---

5. The following discussion summarizes our study entitled "Jésus, le prophète par excellence, d'après Jean 10,24-39", which appeared in *Neues Testament und Kirche. Für Rudolf Schnackenburg*, Joachim Gnilka ed., 1974, pp. 160-171.

6. See the *midrash* on Ps 82 (W.G. BRAUDE, *The Midrash on Psalms*, Yale Judaica Series, xiii, 2, New Haven, 1959, p. 59). See also *Sotah* 47b; *Sanh* 6b-7a.

of his judiciary powers were transferred to "chiefs" (1:15; cf. Ps 82:7), who thus became the first "judges" charged with adjudicating disputes among the Hebrews. Behind the "judges" of whom psalm 82 speaks one can discern the person of Moses, the "judge" *par excellence*.

Now Jesus uses, in his reasoning, expressions which evoke rather clearly the prophetic mission. The words he speaks in verses 35-36 are taken from Jer 1:4-7:

John 10:35-36	Jer 1:4, 5b, 7
εἰ ἐκείνους εἶπεν θεοὺς πρὸς οὓς	
ὁ λόγος τοῦ θεοῦ ἐγένετο	καὶ ἐγένετο λόγος τοῦ κυρίου πρός με λέγων·... καὶ πρὸ τοῦ σε ἐξελθεῖν ἐκ μήτρας
... ὃν ὁ πατὴρ ἡγίασεν καὶ	ἡγίακά σε... πρὸς πάντας
ἀπέστειλεν εἰς τὸν κόσμον...	οὓς ἐὰν ἐξαποστείλω σε πορεύσῃ
If he calls gods those to whom the word of God was addressed...	and the word of the Lord was addressed to me, saying... ... and before you left your mother's womb
... He whom the Father consecrated	I consecrated you ... Toward all those
and sent into the world...	to whom I will send you you will go

The prophetic mission of Jesus is clearly evoked in this text, with reference to that of Jeremiah. But we have seen that Jeremiah described this prophetic mission referring to that of Moses by taking up the terms found in Deut 18:15-18. It is the same in the gospel according to John. At the beginning (10:25) and at the end (10:37-38) of his discussion with the Jews, he points to the "works" he has accomplished in his Father's name and which witness to the fact that he was indeed sent by God. In the same way, Moses had to accomplish three "signs" to authenticate his mission. By putting such words into the mouth of Jesus, the evangelist, in line with Jewish tradition, identified the "judges" spoken of in psalm 82 with the prophets of the Old Testament, especially Moses. Twice, moreover, the book of Exodus makes Moses equivalent to a god (Exod 4:16; 7:1).

It is now easy to understand the reasoning of Jesus. He responds to the Jews by referring to himself in the manner of speaking of the Old Testament. Certain texts in the Bible give to men — especially the "judges", of whom Moses was as the archetype — the title "gods", that is to say, "sons of God". This title does not imply, therefore, any pretension to make oneself into "God", in the transcendent meaning. Why then would the Jews accuse Jesus of having blasphemed because he called himself "son of God"?

Echoes of this discussion between Jesus and the Jews are heard at the trial of Jesus before the Sanhedrin, especially in its Lucan form. In this tenth chapter of John, verses 24b-25a have their equivalent in Luke 22:67, and the verses 33-36 in Luke 22:70. The theme of blasphemy is taken from Mark 14:64 and Matt 26:65 (and was omitted by Luke)[7]. The gospel of John is telling us that the Sanhedrin condemned Jesus to death for blasphemy because he called himself son of God before them. But where is the blasphemy in that? The Jewish authorities therefore condemned Jesus unjustly, for a so-called blasphemy.

II. THE ONLY-BEGOTTEN

Jesus is not simply "son of God". He is also the "Only-begotten" (μονογενής). After having defined the meaning of this expression, which only the Johannine writings apply to Christ, we shall see its meaning in the Gospel of John, and especially in the Prologue.

1. *The Meaning of the Word*

The general meaning of this word presents no difficulty. It is composed of the adjective (μόνος), which signifies "only, single", and what one could consider a verbal adjective (γενής), derived from the verb (γεννᾶν), which signifies "to beget". In fact, although the expression corresponds to the English "only child", we have rendered it by "Only-begotten" to note the difference with the word υἱός used in the title "son of God". In Judg 11:34, it is said of the daughter of Jephthah that she was "his only daughter (μονογενής),

---

7. See M.-É. BOISMARD-A. LAMOUILLE, *Synopsis Graeca Quattuor Evangeliorum*, Leuven-Paris, 1986, p. 280.

and apart from her, he had neither son nor daughter". It is the same with Sarah, the fiancée of Tobiah; she says: "I am the only daughter (μονογενής) of my father, and he has no other child" (Tob 3: 15). In the New Testament, it is the word which is used for the only son of the widow of Nain (Luke 7: 12), the only daughter of Jairus (Luke 8: 42) or the epileptic child (Luke 9: 38). Similarly in Heb 11: 17 Isaac is the only son of Abraham.

One sees immediately that this term μονογενής, said of Christ, places him in a privileged position in his relationship with God, unique compared with other men. All just men can be called "sons of God", but Jesus alone is the Only-begotten son of God. We will next attempt to explain why.

2. *The Logos is the Only-Begotten*

a) It is by his humanity, as we have just seen, that Jesus is the "son of God". On the other hand, if he is the "Only-begotten", it is as the Logos incarnate. The evidence of this is found in the Prologue. It is the same person who is called Logos in the first part of the Prologue (John 1: 1-14), then Only-begotten son in the second part (1: 14-18). Verse 14 makes the connection between the two titles: "The Logos became flesh and dwelt among us, and we have beheld his glory, glory that he has from the Father as the Only-begotten Son, full of grace and truth". The Logos is none other than the Only-begotten son.

We return in fact to a theme known in sapiential literature. In Prov 8: 23-25, Wisdom proclaims: "Ages ago I was set up, at the first (ἐν ἀρχῇ), before the beginning of the earth. When there were no depths... I was brought forth (γεννᾷ με)". It can be said of the Logos as of Wisdom that he was begotten by God. He has "come out of the mouth" of God (Isa 55: 11; cf. Deut 8: 3 LXX), just as Wisdom can say, "I have come out of the mouth of the Most-High" (Sir 24: 3). It is this "coming out" of the mouth of God which is considered as childbirth, both for the Logos as well as for Wisdom.

b) But the evangelist seeks to set himself apart from the sapiential books on one essential point. Even if she is "begotten by God", Wisdom remains a creature. This is said explicitly in Prov 8: 22: "The Lord created me (ἔκτισέν με) at the beginning of his work". One reads the same thing in Sir 24: 8: "Then the Creator of all things instructed me, and he who created me (ὁ κτίσας με) had me plant my tent". Creation would seem, then, to have been completed in two phases. God first created Wisdom, coming out of his mouth as if she were begotten by Him. Then he created the cosmos through Wisdom, having as it were his eyes fixed on her. The evangelist, for his part, refuses this idea of a Logos created by God, and that is why, we think, he added to verse 1 of the Prologue the clause "and the Logos was God" (καὶ θεὸς ἦν ὁ λόγος). Since the Logos is God, it cannot have been created. The Logos is therefore the "Only-begotten son" by virtue of a relationship *ad intra*, to use a term from Scholastic theology. If the term Logos is put in relation to God, the term "Only-begotten son" refers to the Father: "The Only-begotten Son, who is in the bosom of the Father, he has made him known" (John 1:18). God is both "Father" and "Son".

c) It is also on this important point that the Johannine Logos distinguishes itself from the Logos of Philo[8]. For the Alexandrian philosopher, the Logos is an intermediary between God and the cosmos. God cannot be in immediate contact with the creature. He therefore created the cosmos through the intermediary of the Logos. Was the Logos God? In spite of certain texts sometimes cited to suggest this, it was impossible. Otherwise, one would have to say that God was in direct relation with the cosmos. The Logos is situated rather on the side of the creature. On several occasions Philo gives it the title "First-born" (πρωτόγονος)[9], but this primacy is said in relation to the cosmos which itself is the "second-born son" (νεώτερος υἱός)[10]. It is possible that John brings together these two titles "Logos" and "Only-begotten son" under the influence of Philo. But one sees a difference: for Philo, the Logos is not God; for John, the Logos is God, and his divine birth is "unique".

3. *The Manifestation of the Only-Begotten*

In the Prologue of the gospel of John, the Logos is not called the Only-begotten son until after mention of the incarnation (verse 14). Until verse 14a, it is only a matter of God and of his Logos, while after verse 14b the couplet Father/Only-begotten son appears (verses

8. See J. LEBRETON, *Histoire du dogme de la Trinité*, tome I, Paris, 1927[6], pp. 209-251. M.-J. LAGRANGE, "Vers le Logos de saint Jean", in *RB* 32 (1923) 161-184; 321-371.

9. *De Agric.* 51 — *De Confus. Ling.* 63.146 — *De Somn.* I 315.

10. *De Ebriet.* 30. Compare this to the hymn cited by Paul in Col 1:15 in which Christ is said to be πρωτότοκος πασῆς κτίσεως.

14b, 18). To understand this evolution of themes, the narrative of the Transfiguration as it is recounted in the Synoptics (Matt 17:1-8; Mark 9:2-8; Luke 9:28-36) must be analyzed.

As many commentators have recognized, this narrative makes reference to the theophany of the Sinai witnessed by Moses, according to Exod 33–34 (cf. Exod 24). Both scenes take place on the summit of a moutain. Note the same formula "he went up the moutain" (ἀνέβη εἰς τὸ ὄρος) in Luke 9:28b and Exod 34:4 or 24:15. Jesus goes up in the company of three of his disciples. In Exod 34, Moses goes up alone, but in 24:13 he is accompanied by his servant Joshua. While Moses speaks with God "the skin of his face shone" (Exod 34:29-30); the same is said of Jesus: "His face shone like the sun" (Matt 17:2; cf. Luke 9:29). In both theophanies, the divine presence is manifested by the appearance of a cloud (Exod 34:5; Matt 17:5 et par.). The formula in Matthew and Luke, "a cloud... overshadowed them" (νεφέλη ἐπεσκίασεν αὐτούς) takes up the formula from Exod 40:35; when the tent of meeting is set up, God manifests his presence in the same way: Moses cannot enter into the tent because "the cloud took him under its shadow" (ἐπεσκίαζεν ἐπ᾽ αὐτὴν ἡ νεφέλη). In the narrative of the Transfiguration, a voice is heard from the center of the cloud: "This is my beloved son, listen to him". The order that is given recalls the promise concerning the sending of a prophet similar to Moses, in Deut 18:15: "The Lord your God will raise up for you a prophet like me from among you, from your brethren, and you will listen to him". This theme forms, in fact, the conclusion of the theophany of Sinai: Moses speaks with God, then he transmits to the Israelites the orders which he received from Him (Exod 34:34).

The narrative of the Transfiguration thus seeks to evoke, with regard to Jesus, the theophany of Sinai witnessed by Moses according to Exod 33-34. But we have seen that verses 14-18 of the Prologue were themselves also written with reference to this same theophany of Sinai. Is it not therefore legitimate to think that these verses of the Prologue were written against a backdrop of the narrative of the Transfiguration? Certain literary clues confirm that it is. In John 1:14, it is said: "... and we have seen his glory". Similarly, in Luke 9:32, we learn that the disciples "saw his glory", that of Jesus transfigured. In John 1:14, this glory is "like the glory that the *Only-begotten son* receives from the Father"; in the Synoptics, a voice comes from the cloud saying: "This is my *beloved* son".

But in the Greek of the Old Testament, the two terms μονογενής and ἀγαπητός are interchangeable and both translate the same word in Hebrew: יחיד. In fact, the term ἀγαπητός is often used to designate an only son (Gen 22:2, 12, 16; Amos 8:10; Zech 12:10).

The connection between John 1:14 and the scene of the Transfiguration is confirmed by the text of 2 Pet 1:16-17. The author of this epistle, who identifies himself with the apostle Peter, alludes to the Transfiguration in these terms, which are interesting to place in parallel with John 1:14:

John 1:14	2 Peter 1:16-17
καὶ ἐθεασάμεθα τὴν δόξαν αὐτοῦ, δόξαν ὡς μονογενοῦς παρὰ πατρός...	ἀλλ' ἐπόπται γενηθέντες τῆς ἐκείνου μεγαλειότητος. λαβὼν γὰρ παρὰ θεοῦ πατρὸς τιμὴν καὶ δόξαν, φωνῆς ἐνεχθείσης αὐτῷ τοιᾶσδε ὑπὸ τῆς μεγαλοπρεποῦς δόξης· ὁ υἱός μου ὁ ἀγαπητός μου οὗτός ἐστιν...
and we have seen his glory, glory as of the Only-begotten Son	... but having been eye-witnesses of his majesty.
from the Father...	receiving in fact from God the Father honor and glory, as a voice came to him from the bosom of the majestic glory: "This is my Son, my Beloved..."

One sees here clearly the equivalence between the titles "Only-begotten son" and "beloved".

The text of John 1:14-18 therefore alludes to the narrative of Exod 33–34 and to that of the Transfiguration of Jesus. Now it is at the Transfiguration that God solemnly declares about Jesus in the presence of his disciples: "This is my beloved son". The title "beloved" or "Only-begotten son" — and let us remember that these two terms are practically identical in the Old Testament — were revealed to the disciples at the time of the Transfiguration, and therefore after the incarnation of the Word. Now we understand why, in the Prologue, it does not appear until after mention of the incarnation.

CHAPTER FIVE

THE MOMENT OF THE INCARNATION

It is said in John 1:14, "And the Logos became flesh". The word "flesh" does not designate the body, as opposed to the soul. According to a common way of speaking in the Old Testament, it designates everything that is corruptible compared to the incorruptible and eternal God: "All flesh is grass, and all its beauty is like the flower of the field. The grass withers, the flower fades, when the breath of the Lord blows upon it... The grass withers, the flower fades; but the word of our God will stand forever" (Is 40:6-8). Here, the word "flesh" designates humanity as that which is corruptible, as in this text from Genesis: "My spirit shall not abide in man for ever, for he is flesh, but his days shall be a hundred and twenty years" (Gen 6:3). This meaning is well known also to the author of the fourth Gospel (John 17:2; cf. 3:6).

So the Logos became a corruptible man. But at what moment was such an "incarnation" accomplished? Spontaneously one wants to place the realization of this mystery at the time of the conception of Jesus. But an analysis of the Synoptic narrative of the baptism of Jesus will demonstrate that the answer to this question is not obvious.

1. *The Baptism of Jesus*

The baptism of Jesus is recounted in the three Synoptics (Mark 1:9-11; Matt 3:13-17; Luke 3:21-22). John alludes to it without recounting the scene (John 1:32-34). According to the Marcan narrative, whose formulation is the most archaic, Jesus sees the Spirit descend on him and hears a voice from the heavens saying, "You are my son, my beloved, with you I am well pleased". The celestial voice takes up the oracle of Isaiah 42:1: "Behold my servant (ὁ παῖς μου) whom I uphold, my chosen, in whom my soul delights. I have put my spirit upon him..."[1]. In Greek, the word παῖς means both "son" and "servant". In the narrative of Mark (cf.

---

1. The reference to Isa 42:1 is certain. Compare Matt 3:17 to Matt 12:18, which again cites Isa 42:1 in a form analogous to 3:17.

Matt), the meaning "son" was opted for, and the word υἱός employed, which presents no ambiguity. As to the coming of the Spirit, it fulfills three prophecies of the Old Testament concerning the Messiah: first, Isa 42:1, but also Isa 11:2 and Isa 61:1.

Now in Isa 11:1-2 we read, "There shall come forth a shoot from the stump of Jesse, and a branch shall grow out of his roots. And the Spirit of the Lord shall rest upon him, the spirit of wisdom and understanding, the spirit of counsel and might, the spirit of knowledge and the fear of the Lord". Jesse was the father of David. We are therefore concerned here with a messianic king. He will receive the Spirit, which is above all the "spirit of wisdom and understanding" (πνεῦμα σοφίας καὶ συνέσεως), qualities he will need in order to govern his people. In this way king Solomon, at the time of the dream he had at Gibeon, asked God to give him not riches but "an understanding mind to govern thy people" (1 Kgs 3:9). And God replied: "Behold, I now do according to your word. Behold, I give you a wise and discerning mind (καρδίαν φρονίμην καὶ σοφήν) so that none like you has been before you and none like you shall arise after you" (3:12). In the Book of Wisdom, Solomon is thought to make the same prayer to God. In order to be able to govern his people well, he asks, "God of our Fathers and Lord of mercy, who by your word have made the universe, and in your wisdom have fitted human beings to rule the creatures that you have made, to govern the world in holiness and justice and in honesty of soul to dispense fair judgment, grant me Wisdom (σοφίαν), consort of your throne, and do not reject me from the number of your children" (Wis 9:1-4). It is apparent that Wisdom tends to be identified with the Spirit, as in Wis 9:17: "And who could ever have known your will, had you not given Wisdom and sent your holy Spirit from above?". In any case, there is no wisdom without Spirit.

2. *The Spirit and Jesus*

Jesus therefore received the Spirit at the time of his baptism. From then on, it is the Spirit making him act. This is especially underscored in the Gospel of Luke. Immediately after the scene of the baptism, he writes: "And Jesus, full of the Holy Spirit, returned from the Jordan, and was led by the Spirit for forty days in the wilderness, tempted by the devil" (Luke 4:1-2). It is therefore due to the Spirit that Jesus can put an end to the subtle traps laid for him by the devil (cf. 4:13). Jesus returns thereafter to Galilee "by the power of the Spirit", and he begins to teach to the amazement of everyone (4:14-15). It is clearly a "spirit of wisdom" which he received. When he comes to Nazareth, he enters the synagogue, opens the book of the prophet Isaiah and comes to this passage: "The Spirit of the Lord is upon me, because he has anointed me to announce good news to the poor...". Jesus explains that this Scripture has just been fulfilled, and all are in admiration before "the gracious words which proceeded out of his mouth" (Luke 4:16-22). Luke does not speak here of "wisdom", but the theme is implicit. It is made explicit in the parallel passages in Matthew and Mark: "What is this wisdom given to him?" (Mark 6:2b; cf. Matt 13:54). Later he teaches in the synagogue of Capharnaum and the listeners "were astonished at his teaching, for his word was with authority" (Luke 4:31-32). His words are so effective that he can make demons obey him (4:36) and command fevers (4:39). This entire sequence ends with this confession by the demons he is throwing out: "You are the son of God", a confession which refers back to the scene of the baptism, where the celestial voice said to him, "You are my son, today I have begotten you" (3:22b).

3. The Meaning of the Scene of the Baptism of Jesus

We see then that for Luke, it is at the time of his baptism that Jesus received the Spirit which took possession of him, made him act, permitted him to vanquish the devil and all the demons, conferred on him a wisdom which allowed him to teach the crowds in Galilee with full authority, and gave his word a power analogous to God's. One is forced to conclude from this that when the celestial voice declared to him, "You are my son, *today* I have begotten you", it was affirming that Jesus *was made "son of God"* at the time of his baptism, because of the Spirit which he had just received. Everything leads one to believe that the viewpoint is identical in the parallel narratives of Mark and Matthew. After having given the Spirit to Jesus, God affirms to him, "You are my son, the beloved (ὁ ἀγαπητός)" (Mark 1:11; cf. Matt 3:17).

But if, according to the Synoptic tradition, it is at the time of his baptism that Jesus was made the "beloved son" of God, the inevitable question is this: In the gospel of John, at what moment is the Logos incarnated in Jesus? At what moment does Jesus become the Only-begotten son (ὁ μονογενὴς), since, as we have said, there is an equivalence between the titles "beloved" and "Only-begotten on"?

4. *A Lucan Transposition*

Before answering this question, let us see how it is posed in the Lucan tradition. In Luke 1:35, in the narrative of the annunciation, the angel declares to Mary:

πνεῦμα ἅγιον ἐπελεύσεται ἐπὶ σέ,
καὶ δύναμις ὑψίστου ἐπισκιάσει σοι,
διὸ καὶ τὸ γεννώμενον ἅγιον κληθήσεται υἱὸς θεοῦ

The Holy Spirit will come upon you,
and the power of the Most High will overshadow you;
therefore the holy being to be born will be called "son of God".

The two essential components of the narrative of the baptism of Jesus are found in this "annunciation to Mary". Due to the coming of the Holy Spirit, he who will be born of Mary will be called "son of God". Luke has therefore effected the following transposition; it is not at the time of his baptism that Jesus became "son of God", but rather at the moment of his conception. And it is in line with this transposition that he tells us of Jesus that "the child grew and became strong, *full of wisdom*, and the favor of God was upon him" (2:40). He then relates the episode of Jesus discussing in the Temple with the doctors of the Law (as he will do later in the synagogue in Nazareth), and he notes: "All who heard him were amazed at his understanding and his anwers" (2:47). Luke finally tells us a second time: "And Jesus increased *in wisdom*, grace and stature before God and men" (2:52). Jesus was filled with wisdom from his infancy, and not merely after his baptism, since he had been conceived by the Holy Spirit[2].

5. *The Moment of the Incarnation according to the Prologue of John*

According to the Prologue of the Gospel of John, Jesus is the Only-begotten son inasmuch as he is Logos/Wisdom. In addition, this Logos/Wisdom becomes "flesh", in other words becomes incarnate. But at what moment is this incarnation effected, at the time of

2. The theme of the virgin conception imposes itself as a theological consequence: "How can this be, since I do not known man?" asks Mary of the angel (Lk 1:23).

the baptism of Jesus or at his conception in Mary's womb? If one keeps to the Johannine texts, it is not easy to give an answer to this question.

a) A negative argument allows one to think that, for John, the incarnation would have been effected at the conception of Jesus. In his Gospel, he minimized the Christological implications of the baptismal scene. First, it is no longer Jesus who sees the Spirit descend upon him in the form of a dove, as in Mark 1:10 and Matt 3:16, but rather John the Baptist who attests to having seen the Spirit down upon Jesus (John 1:32, 34). In addition, there is no longer a celestial voice saying to Jesus "You are my Son", as in Mark 1:11 and Luke 3:22. It is the Baptist who attests before the crowd that Jesus is "the Elect[3] of God"; it is no longer even a question of giving the title "Son" to Jesus. The evangelist has completely eliminated from the scene of the baptism everything which could lead to an adoptionist interpretation.

b) There is also a positive argument which leads one to believe that, for John, the incarnation was affected at the conception of Jesus. But it only has value for those who accept, in 1:13, the singular reading of "he who... was begotten". We will not take up a discussion of this problem over which so much ink has already flowed. We will simply explain how the singular reading favors the idea that, for the evangelist, the incarnation was effected at the conception of Jesus.

We would have therefore, in verses 12-13, the following text: "To all who received him, he gave power to become children of God, *he who*, neither of blood, nor of the will of man, nor of the will of the flesh, but of God *was begotten*". Reading this in the plural, the negative part of verse 13, with its three redundant terms, is difficult to justify. It can be easily explained, on the contrary, by a singular reading. Jesus was begotten, not as other men, but "of God". Was there not a danger of assimilating this extraordinary conception with that of those hybrid beings of which the Bible speaks? The Nephilim ("Titans") in Gen 6:1-5, for instance, came from the union between the "sons of God", that is to say the angels, and the "daughters of

---

3. This reading is attested by P⁵ ℵ *pc* b e ff² Syr^SC Amb Aug, and also by a and Sah, which have a double reading. The reading "Son of God" is due to a harmonization with the Synoptics.

men". This theme is taken up again in the book of Enoch (15:4)[4]. This patriarch reproaches the fallen angels, who had dealings with the daughters of men:

ἐν τῷ αἵματι γυναικῶν ἐμιάνθητε
καὶ ἐν αἵματι σαρκὸς ἐγεννήσατε
καὶ ἐν αἵματι ἀνθρώπων ἐπεθυμήσατε

in the blood of women you polluted yourselves
and in the blood of the flesh were you begotten
and in the blood of men you have lusted

The relationship with the Johannine text is obvious. The evangelist, who knew this text or a related text echoing the same traditions, wishes to react against a possible assimilation of the conception of Jesus with that of the Giants of which Genesis speaks. Jesus was begotten not as the Nephilim Giants were, from fallen angels, but "of God".

Thus verse 13 of the Prologue says explicitly that Jesus became the Only-begotten son, not at the time of his baptism, but at the moment of his conception in the womb of Mary.

4. The connection between this passage of the book of Enoch and John 1:13 was also pointed out by Peter HOFRICHTER, *Nicht aus Blut sondern monogen aus Gott geboren* (Forsch. z. Bibel, 31), Würzburg, 1978, pp. 95ff.

CHAPTER SIX

JESUS IS GOD

Let us analyze now the Johannine passages in which Jesus is identified with God. These are of two kinds. There are, on the one hand, the texts in which Jesus attributes to himself the formula "I am", used in an absolute fashion, as if it were a proper noun, and on the other hand the texts in which the title "God" is applied to Jesus.

I. THE FORMULA "I AM"

The phrase "I am" appears frequently in the Gospel of John. But it can have very different implications according to the manner in which it is used.

1. *Weak Meaning*

Such a construction often assumes no special meaning: the verb "to be" simply plays the copulative role between a subject and its attribute. When Jesus affirms "I am the bread of life" (6:35; 48), "I am the light of the world" (8:12), "I am the door" (10:7; 9), "I am the good Shepherd" (10:11; 14), "I am the resurrection and the life" (11:25), "I am the way, the truth and the life" (14:6), the phrases he utters in this manner present no grammatical peculiarity. Solely from the stylistic point of view, this construction is of some interest since it evokes, it seems, the *pesher* style of the Jewish tradition so well represented in the Qumran texts. The example given in 6:35, 48 is especially instructive on this point. Such stylistic considerations are not relevant to our purpose, however, and we will therefore not pause over them.

2. *Strong Meaning*

It is a completely different matter when this construction is used in an absolute manner.

a) A first case is given in John 8:58. At the end of a discussion with the Jews, Jesus declares to them:

πρὶν ᾿Αβραὰμ γενέσθαι ἐγώ εἰμι
Before Abraham became, I am

To the "became" of Abraham is opposed the "exist" of Jesus, expressed in an atemporal present. This phrase suggests not only the pre-existence of Jesus vis-à-vis Abraham, but also existence in a certain absolute sense. One thinks of God's revelation of his name to Moses in the episode of the burning bush: "I am who I am" (Exod 3:14). In the present text of Exodus, the second "I am" must be understood as a proper noun, since God adds, "Say this to the people of Israel, 'I am' has sent me to you...".

b) But the construction "I am" is used in a stranger way in a series of three texts which each offer the same grammatical peculiarity:

8:24 ἐὰν γὰρ μὴ *πιστεύσητε ὅτι ἐγώ εἰμι* ἀποθανεῖσθε...
13:19 ἀπ᾿ ἄρτι λέγω ὑμῖν πρὸ τοῦ γενέσθαι ἵνα *πιστεύσητε ὅταν γένηται ὅτι ἐγώ εἰμι*
8:28 ὅταν ὑψώσητε τὸν υἱὸν τοῦ ἀνθρώπου τότε *γνώσεσθε ὅτι ἐγώ εἰμι*

8:24 if you *do not believe that I am*, you will die in your sins
13:19 from now I tell you this, before it takes place, so that when (it) does take place, *you will believe that I am*
8:28 when you have lifted up the Son of man, then *you will know that I am*

In these three texts, the construction «I am» is used absolutely, but as part of an object clause depending in the verbs «believe» and «know». One is almost tempted to translate not «that I am» but «who I am», and some have seen in this an error in translation from the Aramaic original, since in that language the same element די can play the role of a relative pronoun as well as that of a declarative conjunction. But is it likely that a translator from Aramaic into Greek would have made the same mistake in three different passages?

In fact, these three Jesus texts echo Isa 43:10, read in the LXX:

למען תדעו ותאמינו לי ותבינו כי אני הוא
ἵνα *γνῶτε* καὶ *πιστεύσητε* καὶ *συνῆτε ὅτι ἐγώ εἰμι*
... that *you know* and *believe* and understand *that I am*

As in the Johannine texts, the construction "I am" is used absolutely and in an object clause which depends upon the verbs "know" and "believe". The literary borrowing is certain. We must therefore analyze the meaning of this construction in Isaiah.

c) We read in Isa 45:18:

כי כה אמר יהוה בורא השמים ... אני יהוה ואין עוד

οὕτως λέγει κύριος ὁ ποιήσας τὸν οὐρανόν... ἐγώ εἰμι καὶ οὐκ ἔστιν ἔτι
thus speaks the Lord who made the heavens... I am, and there is no other

In this text, the construction ἐγώ εἰμι, "I am", translates an original Hebrew אני יהוה. The meaning is therefore "I (am) Yahweh". This construction also introduces a very clear monotheistic affirmation: "... and there is no other".

In the text of Isa 43:10-11, cited above in connection with some Johannine passages, the construction ἐγώ εἰμι translates the Hebrew אני הוא, which can be rendered "It is I". God announces the liberation of his people, who can recognize that "It is Yahweh" who has effected this liberation. The rest of the text is an affirmation of monotheism: "... before me, there was no other God, and there will be none after me". Isaiah then returns to the theme of the saving God: "I (am) God (ἐγὼ ὁ θεός — יהוה אנכי) and outside of me there is no savior".

Beside these texts of Isaiah, Deut 32:39 should also be cited:

ראו עתה כי אני אני הוא ואין אלהים עמדי

ἴδετε ἴδετε ὅτι ἐγώ εἰμι καὶ οὐκ ἔστιν θεὸς πλὴν ἐμοῦ
Behold, behold, that I am, and there is no other God than I.

Note here again how the construction "I am" is immediately followed by the most absolute possible affirmation of monotheism.

In summary, the Greek expression ἐγώ εἰμι corresponds to two Hebrew constructions which mean either "I (am) Yahweh", or "I am (Yahweh)". It therefore implies either explicitly or implicitly the name of Yahweh, "He is", which reflects the revelation God made of himself to Moses: "I am who I am" (Exod 3:14). When God speaks, he calls himself "I am". When men speak of God, they call him "He is". In addition, this construction is always followed by an affirmation of monotheism.

d) According to the Gospel of John therefore, when Jesus applies the construction "I am" to himself, in a fairly clear reference to the

text of Isa 43:10, he speaks as God spoke in the Old Testament.
More to the point, he claims for himself this name of Yahweh which
was the proper name of God, revealed to Moses in the episode of the
burning bush. Since the construction "I am" in the Old Testament is
always followed by an affirmation of monotheism, Jesus is not
claiming to be any other god than God. On the contrary, he lets it
be understood that God and he are one single God.

e) It is obviously in this way that the action of the arrest scene of
Jesus (John 18:4-6) must be understood. Jesus goes before those
who have come to arrest him and asks, "Whom do you seek?". They
answer him, "Jesus the Nazarean". He says to them, "I am (He)"
(ἐγώ εἰμι). At that moment, all draw back and fall to the ground.
The expression "I am (He)" has two meanings for the evangelist. It
is of course the direct answer of Jesus to the question which he had
just been asked. But this answer evokes the Name which Jesus had
claimed in his discussions with the Jews. And his adversaries are
suddenly overwhelmed by the mere mention of this Name.

II. JESUS IS GOD

In the texts which we have just analyzed, Jesus is only identified
with God in a veiled fashion. But other, clearer passages exist in
which the actual title "God" is applied to Christ. These are the cases
we must examine now. We will see that such an attribution to Jesus
of the title "God" was not made without some serious difficulties.

1. *The Word is God*

Let us see first the beginning of the Prologue of the Gospel,
remembering what we said in commenting on John 1:1-2. We
distinguished two redactional levels in this text. There was, first, an
ancient hymn, probably pre-Johannine, with this tenor: "In the
beginning was the Word and the Word was with God". The
evangelist added to this the end of verse 1 and the redactional
summary consisting of verse 2. What is important in this addition is
obviously the end of verse 1: "... and the Word was God". It is
immediately obvious that this addition, from the point of view of
our human logic, introduces a contradiction into the text. The Word

is both distinct from God, since it is said that it is "with God", as well as identical to God, since it is said to be God. Did the evangelist glimpse that this would later become the very foundation of Trinitarian doctrine, a distinction in God expressed in human terms between "nature" and "person"? It would be difficult to say so. We must nevertheless recognize that the Johannine text, as it was written by the evangelist, requires the theologian to reflect on the mystery of the relationship between the Word and God.

2. *Jesus is God*

Since the Word is God, and the Word was incarnate in Jesus, there was only one more step to take to affirm that Jesus was God. In fact, when Jesus appears to Thomas in the fourth Gospel, the apostle makes this profession of faith: "My Lord and my God" (Jn 20:28). Jesus is therefore the "God" of Thomas. The use of the possessive could suggest that the title "God" should be taken in what could be called a "functional" sense. Jesus is Thomas's "God" in the sense that, saved from death, Jesus would be the principle of salvation for his disciples[1]. But this does not seem to be the case, since in 1 John 5:20, probably by the same author, the title "God" is explicitly given to "Jesus Christ": "We know that the Son of God has come and that he has given us understanding so that we may know the One who is true, and we are in Him who is true, in his Son Jesus Christ, *who is the true God* and eternal life". The demonstrative *who* can only refer to the person of Jesus Christ, mentioned just before. We therefore have the affirmation that Jesus Christ "is the true God"[2].

3. *A Reaction of Refusal*

a) As we shall see, however, such an affirmation was not made in Johannine circles without difficulties. It was even denied in John 17:3, a passage of the Gospel which we believe to be late. This is the problem we now consider.

---

1. Cf. the explanations we presented on pp. 99-105.

2. Attribution of the title "God" to Jesus is rare in the New Testament and is found only in late texts such as Tit 2:13 and 2 Pet 1:1. One should also probably add the doxology of Rom 9:5, although we believe Rom 9-11 to be a deutero-Pauline addition.

Let us place 1 John 5:20 and John 17:3 side by side:

1 Jn 5:20	Jn 17:3
οἴδαμεν ὅτι ὁ υἱός τοῦ θεοῦ	
ἥκει καὶ δέδωκεν ἡμῖν διάνοιαν	
	αὕτη δέ ἐστιν ἡ αἰώνιος ζωὴ
ἵνα γινώσκωμεν	ἵνα γινώσκωμέν σε
τὸν ἀληθινὸν	τὸν μόνον ἀληθινὸν θεὸν
καὶ ἐσμὲν ἐν τῷ ἀληθινῷ	
ἐν τῷ υἱῷ αὐτοῦ	καὶ ὃν ἀπέστειλας
Ἰησοῦ Χριστῷ	Ἰησοῦν Χριστόν
οὗτός ἐστιν ὁ ἀληθινὸς θεὸς	
καὶ ζωὴ αἰώνιος	

We know that the Son of God	
has come and that he has given us	
understanding	
	This is *eternal life*
that we may know	that we know you,
the One who is true	*the one true God.*
and we are in The one who is true,	
in his Son	and him whom you sent,
Jesus Christ	Jesus Christ
he is *the true God*	
and *eternal life.*	

These two texts are certainly interdependent, given the common expressions which are found in them. Note that the construction "the true God" is found nowhere else in the New Testament (cf. however 1 Thess 1:9) and that the name "Jesus Christ", relatively frequent in 1 John, is found nowhere else in the Gospel of John except in 1:17.

A certain number of clues lead one to think that it is John 17:3 which depends on 1 Jn 5:20. Note first that, according to most commentators, John 17:3 reads like a gloss inserted into the great prayer of Jesus which constitutes this chapter 17. It goes poorly with the rest of the prayer. Lagrange considered it a gloss by the evangelist inserted into an authentic prayer of Jesus. But two literary clues suggest that John 17:3 is later than 1 John 5:20. The expression "eternal life" is found 17 times in John, six times in 1 John and 12 times in the rest of the New Testament. It ordinarily appears without the article, even when it ought to have it. But John 17:3 is an exception to this rule. In addition, the adjective normally follows the noun. Here again, John 17:3 is an exception to the rule. Jn 17:3 thus offers an expression contrary to the style of John, while in 1 John 5:20 the expression is in perfectly regular form. In 1 John 5:20 the phrase "he has given us understanding that we may know the One who is true", echoes Jer 24:7, "And I will give them a heart to know me, to know that I am the Lord". The phrase was simply Hellenized by replacing "heart" with "understanding". This theme of the "knowledge" of God is explained much better, therefore, in 1 John 5:20 than in John 17:3.

We can therefore assert that John 17:3 depends on 1 John 5:20. It is also clear that Jn 17:3 seeks to deny what 1 John 5:20 affirms. The complete construction "the true God" is no longer said of Jesus. In addition, it is completed by the addition of the adjective "one", which evokes the theme of Jewish monotheism. Finally, the person of "Jesus Christ" is clearly separated from that of the "one true God". As R. Brown[3] has written, "Note that the 'one true God' is not identified with 'Jesus Christ'. This verse seems to go against the other verses in John, which call Jesus "God (1:1, 18; 20:28)". The conclusion is inescapable: John 17:3 seeks to react against the attribution of the title "God" to Jesus. Jesus Christ must be distinguished from God, who remains "the *one* true God".

b) For a mind trained in the Jewish tradition, the attribution to Jesus of the title "God" was difficult to accept. Was this not a fall into ditheism, into the affirmation that there are two "gods"? To escape this danger required the elaboration of a theology which had not yet been done at the end of the first century. A certain number of Jewish-Christians belonging to Johannine circles refused to make that leap, resulting in the schism echoed in 1 John 2:18-19: "Children, it is the last hour and, as you have heard that the Antichrist is coming, so now many Antichrists have appeared. Therefore we know that it is the last hour. They went out from us, but they were not of us. For if they had been of us, they would have continued with us. But they went out so that it might be plain that they all are not of us". In verses 22-23, the author of the epistle makes his thinking explicit: "This is the Antichrist: he who denies the Father and the Son. No one who denies the Son has the Father. He who confesses the Son has the Father also". The term "Son" should be

3. R.E. BROWN, *The Gospel According to John* (The Anchor Bible, 29 and 29A), New York, 1966 and 1970, vol. 2, p. 741.

understood here in a transcendent sense, implying the divinity of
Jesus. Thus those that the author of the epistle calls the Antichrists
separated themselves from their brothers because they refused to
recognize that Jesus was God. Verse 3 was added to the prayer of
Jesus in John 17 by someone who probably belonged to this group.

c) Among the rare texts of the New Testament which give Jesus
the title "God" is Tit 2:13-14: "Awaiting our blessed hope, the
appearing of the glory of our great God and Savior Jesus Christ,
who gave himself for us to redeem us from all iniquity...". One
wonders nevertheless whether or not there was the same negative
reaction to attributing the title "God" to Jesus in Pauline circles as
there was in Johannine ones. 1 Tim 2:6 contains the same allusion
to our redemption by Christ as in Tit 2:14, by Hellenization of
Jesus' saying given in Mark 10:45. These two texts are therefore
related. But we find in 1 Tim 2:5:

> εἷς γὰρ θεὸς
> εἷς καὶ μεσίτης θεοῦ καὶ ἀνθρώπων
> ἄνθρωπος Χριστὸς 'Ιησοῦς
>
> Because one (is) God
> one also the mediator between God and man
> a man, Christ Jesus

This text begins by affirming the principle of Jewish monotheism:
there is only one God. Then, concerning the unique mediator, it calls
attention to the fact that he is a man. There is therefore an
opposition between the one God and the one mediator who is Jesus
Christ, the man.

Note that in all the texts which we have just seen — 1 John 5:20,
John 17:3, Tit 2:13 and 1 Tim 2:5 — Jesus is designated with his
title "Christ". Let us not forget that the Jewish-Christian confession
of faith was "Jesus is the Christ". It would therefore have been in
Jewish-Christian circles that one would have found both the affirmation that Jesus was God and the reaction against such an affirmation
in order to safuegard the Jewish principle of monotheism thought to
be under assault by attributing to Jesus the title "God".

CHAPTER SEVEN

THE EVOLUTION OF CHRISTOLOGY

We have analyzed the theme — and its harmonics — of Jesus as the new Moses, without taking into consideration the redactional levels that we identified in book III of the Synopsis. In finishing this study, we will see how the texts we have examined are divided between these several levels: Document C, John II-A, John II-B and possibly John III. We will then be able to see if Johannine Christology evolved and, if so, in what direction.

A. *Document C*

Jesus, the Prophet similar to Moses

At the level of Document C, Christology consisted essentially of the presentation of Jesus as a new Moses, implicitly referring to the text of Deut 18:18. To accomplish his aim, the author proceeded in a rather subtle manner. It is the narratives themselves which, by their nature or by a few short allusions, turn the reader's thought toward the theme of Jesus the new Moses.

The first group of these narratives includes the witness of John the Baptist, followed by the calling of Philip and Nathanael. John denies being the Prophet announced by Deut 18:18 (1:19, 21). Why then does he baptize if he is not the Prophet (1:25)? In order to reveal to Israel the Lamb of God, recognized through the descent of the Spirit on Jesus (1:26; 31-32; 29). Then, at the time of the calling of Philip and Nathanael (1:43-49), Jesus was implicitly designated as the Prophet announced by Deut 18:18 and as the King of Israel (cf. also 12:12-13), heir of the royalty of his ancestor, the patriarch Joseph. It therefore answered the expectations of the Samaritan tradition, which glorified Moses the Prophet and Joseph the King.

The second group of narratives included a series of three "signs" performed by Jesus in Galilee at the beginning of his ministry: the water changed into wine at Cana in Galilee (2:1-12), the healing of the son of the royal official at Capharnaum (4:46-54), and the miraculous catch in the sea of Galilee (21:1-14). The link between the first two signs was established in 2:12, the link between the last two by 7:1, 3-4, 6, 9. After having been "revealed" by John the Baptist as sent from God, Jesus "revealed himself" (2:11; 7:3-4; 21:1, 4) through these three signs performed in Galilee. And he revealed himself as a new Moses because it was Moses who first had had to perform three "signs" in order to be recognized by his brothers as having been sent by God (Exod 4:1-9).

The last narrative was found in 19:17-18. Jesus, his arms extended on the cross between two other victims, resembles Moses giving victory to the Hebrews (cf. John 12:31-32), his arms extended, and supported on either side by Aaron and Hur (Exod 17:8-13).

In all of the narratives the allusions to the theme of Jesus the new Moses remained unobtrusive. The Baptist denied being "the Prophet" announced by Deut 18:18, which implied that it was Jesus who was this Prophet. A succession of titles was given to Jesus: "He of whom Moses wrote in the Law", "son of Joseph", "king of Israel". These titles identified him as the heir of the two principal biblical personages venerated by the Samaritans[1]. A series of three "signs" performed in Galilee showed Jesus acting as Moses had in Egypt. Finally, the fact of dying with his arms outstretched, between two others similarly crucified, symbolized Jesus as the victor over the powers of evil, as once Moses had obtained victory over the Amalekites. A few words, a few "signs", a position at the moment of death: these were sufficient to the readers of the Gospel to understand what the author of Document C wished to insinuate.

B. *John II-A*

John II-A takes from its source the theme of Jesus as the prophet similar to Moses but enriches it with a new harmonic: Jesus is much more than Moses because the Wisdom of God is incarnate in him.

1. *Jesus, the Prophet similar to Moses*

John II-A developed the theme of Jesus the new Moses by adding the episode of the multiplication of the loaves (6:1-15). In the

---

1. We do not think that the author of Document C was himself a Samaritan. The narrative of the conversation between Jesus and the Samaritan woman, whose kernel comes from Document C, is written to appeal to the Samaritans but from a perspective which nevertheless criticizes their syncretism.

redaction of the narrative itself, several details orient the reader toward the precedent of Elisha (2 Kings 4:42-44). But in its conclusion, John II-A alludes to the text of Deut 18:18 by having the people — astonished by a miracle reminiscent of that of manna in the desert — exclaim, "This is truly the Prophet who is to come into the world" (6:14). It is therefore John II-A which, for the first time, applies this title in a positive fashion to Jesus.

We have said that this title had a Samaritan flavor about it. John II-A corrected this Samaritan orientation in the narratives of Document C, seen as too exclusive, by coupling this title with that of "Christ" from the Jewish tradition. John II-A is at the origin of the double confession of faith of 7:40-42: "This is truly the Prophet... This is the Christ...". In the same way, at the level of Document C, the narrative of the calling of the first disciples included only verses 43-49, with the affirmation of Philip to Nathanael at its center: "He of whom Moses wrote in the Law (...), we have found..." (1:45). It was, as we have seen, an allusion to the text of Deut 18:18 concerning the coming of the Prophet similar to Moses. John II-A completed this narrative by adding the calling of Andrew and Peter (verses 36-42), analogous in structure and having at its center the affirmation of Andrew to his brother: "We have found the Messiah, the Christ" (1:41). The author of John II-A therefore "Judaized" a Gospel which he judged too exclusively oriented toward the Samaritans.

2. *Jesus, the Wisdom of God*

But John II-A deepened the theme of Jesus the new Moses by adding the theme of Jesus the Wisdom of God. The sapiential books of the Old Testament announced that God would send his Wisdom to men in order to reveal the mysteries of his will to them. For John II-A, this Wisdom came in the person of Jesus.

In order to show this, John II-A uses where appropriate certain literary devices already employed by the author of Document C. Thus, the narrative of the calling of the first disciples (1:36-51) shows Jesus acting as Wisdom was supposed to act (Wis 6:12-16). Above all, John II-A systematized a technique whose precedents are found in the Old Testament: it has Jesus say words which Wisdom itself was supposed to have said in one or another of the sapiential books. It employs what could be called the "imitative" style. Thus

John 14: 21 is a mosaic of reminiscences of texts such as Wis 6: 12, 18, Sir 4: 14 and Prov 8: 17. The use of this technique finds its most perfect expression in the discourse on the bread of life (6: 33-58), where the theme of Jesus as Wisdom is developed from an eschatological perspective. Through Jesus, the ancient curse which weighed on humanity since the offense of our first parents is now lifted, permitting us access to eternal life.

C. *John II-B*

It is the author of John II-B who, illuminated by the Spirit, brings the Christology of the fourth Gospel to its highest point, along the lines already drawn by the author of Document C.

1. *The Prophet like Moses*

The initial theme of Jesus as the new Moses is not forgotten in John II-B. It is even developed by systematizing the "imitative" style technique used in John II-A to show that Jesus was the Wisdom of God. The words of Jesus in John II-B are in fact a mosaic of expressions taken from the Old Testament either concerning Moses, such as Deut 18: 18, or said by Moses, such as Num 16: 28. This was a technique already used by Jeremiah, as we have seen, when he wished to compare himself to Moses. Thus the redaction of texts such as John 12: 48-50, 8: 28-29, 7: 16-17, 17: 8 and others are due to John II-B.

To be more precise, the readers to whom the author of John II-B addresses himself would not have been well versed in the Samaritan ideas concerning the "son of Joseph" and his royal title, to which the author of Document C alluded in John 1: 45, 49. John II-B therefore adds, in the narrative of the wedding feast at Cana, the dialogue between Mary and Jesus reported in John 2: 3-5. We find there the "imitative" style, since in verse 5 Mary say words concerning Jesus recalling those Pharaoh used regarding the patriarch Joseph. For this reason it is clear what meaning should be given to the expressions in verses 45 and 49: Jesus is "the son of Joseph" and also "the king of Israel".

2. *The Wisdom of God*

John II-B developed the theme Jesus-Wisdom very little. We will see why shortly. It is however John II-B who added the words of Jesus in 3:11-13 which refer to Wis 9:16-17 and Bar 3:29. Reference to the theme of Jesus-Wisdom does not otherwise stand out.

3. *The Word of God*

In fact, John II-B is going to fuse the theme of Jesus-Wisdom with that of Jesus-Word of God. He does this in the Prologue of his Gospel. Starting with an ancient hymn to the glory of the creative Word, he develops it through reference to several texts in the sapiential tradition. In Prov 8:22-31, Sir 24:3-34 and Wis 7:22-30, Wisdom praises herself by describing successively her relationship with God, the role she played in creation, her coming into the world, and the benefits she brought to man. This is the schema adopted by John II-B in 1:1-13 by applying it to the Word of God. This application was made that much easier for the author by Isa 55:10-11, a text of sapiential inspiration, which described the Word of God sent to earth to perform among men a work of fertilization before returning to God. This is the general schema of the Prologue. More clearly than John II-A concerning Wisdom, John II-B states moreover that this Word/Wisdom was incarnate in Jesus (1:14).

4. *The Only-Begotten, God*

It is from the angle of the Word that John II-B introduces the theme of the divine sonship of Jesus. Taking an idea already expressed by Philo of Alexandria, John II-B affirms that the Logos is also the Only-begotten son of God. And since the Logos became flesh in Jesus, Jesus is both the Logos of God and the Only-begotten son of God. But, contrary to what Philo of Alexandria thought, the creative Word is both distinct from God and identical to God (1:1-2). One must therefore conclude that Jesus is God. Nowhere in the Gospel does John II-B give Jesus the title "God". This will only be done in the first epistle attributed to John (1 John 5:20). But the author goes perhaps even farther in the Gospel by implying that Jesus may take for himself the Name par excellence: "I am".

D. *John III*

John III did not believe it good to complete the themes inherited from his predecessors. But he did wish to react against this attribution of the title "God" to Jesus. In order to understand his reaction, one must not forget that, as a general rule, he reintroduced into the Gospel themes inherited from Judaism. He is the one who added the theme of the resurrection "on the last day" (cf. in 6:39, 40, 44, 54; 12:48), as well as the echo of the text of Dan 12:2 found in John 5:28-29. He is the one who introduced the phrase "salvation comes from the Jews" in 4:22. We should therefore not be surprised if he believed it necessary to reject the attribution to Jesus of the title "God", which assailed his idea of absolute monotheism. John 17:3, written by him, takes a position against 1 John 5:20. We would be wrong of course to use this text to deny the divinity of Christ. If it was incorporated into the received revelation, it is as a witness of the difficulties encountered, in certain Jewish-Christian circles, by the affirmation that Jesus was God.

Conclusion

a) At the moment of leaving his disciples to return to his Father, Jesus declared to them, "I have yet many things to say to you, but you cannot bear them now. When the Spirit of truth comes, he will guide you into all the truth" (John 16:12-13). In putting these words into the mouth of Jesus, the evangelist is telling us clearly that after the departure of Christ, the Spirit was at work in the Church to finish the revelation of the Truth. It is certain that the apostles, as the good Jews that they were, could not imagine that Jesus was God. They became conscious of it progressively, enlightened by the Spirit, who led them to understand how Jesus had fulfilled in himself the promises contained in the Old Testament. During his lifetime, Jesus was taken for a prophet, reestablishing the prophetic tradition interrupted since the exile in Babylon. But it was quickly understood, and especially in Johannine circles, that Jesus was not simply a prophet, but the Prophet *par excellence*, the new Moses announced by Deut 18:18. It was also understood that in him was incarnated the Wisdom of God that the sapiential books said must come into the world to teach men how to live in accordance with the will of God. And since the Word was God, it was understood that Jesus himself had the right to the title "God", based on this mysterious union between God and Man realized in him.

b) In recognizing an evolution in the Johannine narratives concerning the theme of Jesus the new Moses, it is also possible to resolve an antinomy currently dividing commentators. On the earliest level, that of Document C, it seems clear enough that the author wanted to write a Gospel for the purpose of converting the Samaritans. It proves to them that Jesus fulfills, in his person, their eschatological aspirations. In this sense, Bowman, Freed, Buchanan and the other authors of whom we spoke at the beginning of this study are right. But the reaction of Purvis is also justified: at the later levels, especially that of John II-B, the intention is rather to show the superiority of Jesus over Moses. Can one therefore still speak of a Gospel written for the Samaritans?

INDEX OF BIBLICAL REFERENCES

References in italics refer to fuller analysis.
The asterisk refers to the footnotes.

8:22-30	87.95		9:17	114
8:22-26	71		10:8	78
8:22	108			
8:23-25	108		**Sir**	
8:27-30	71		2:11	97*
8:31	71		2:15-16	78
8:32-36	71		4:11-19	71
9:1-6	71		4:14	73.130
9:5	77		15:3	72.77
11:30	78		24:3ss	131
13:12	78		*24:3-22*	*71*
15:4	78		24:3	71.108
			24:8	77.108
Cant			24:19-21	76
4:2	34		24:21	77
			24:23	70
Wis			43:31	95*
1:13-15	82			
1:16	82.111*		**Isa**	
2:2-3	82.84		11:2	69.114
2:2-3,23	102*		40:6-8	92.113
2:16-20	102		40:6-7	95
2:18	103		42:1	113.113*.114
2:23-24	82		43:10-11	121
2:24	82		43:10	120.122
3:1-4	82.102		45:1	9
3:2	83		45:18	121
4:10	82		55:6	75
6:12-16	129		55:10-11	92.131
6:12	73.76		55:11	108
6:12,18	130		59:21	12
6:14	76		61:1	113
6:16	76		61:1-4	57
6:18	73		66:24	80
7:7	69			
7:17-21	70		**Jer**	
7:22ss	131		1:4,5b,7	106
7:22–9:18	71		1:5ss	1-2
7:26	72		1:7	12
7:28	73		1:9	12
7:29-30	88		5:14	12
9:1-4	114		15:19	85
9:1-2	72.88.89		24:7	125
9:4,10-18	72		36:28	2
9:9	72.87			
9:10	77		**Bar**	
9:13,17	70		3:29	74.131
9:15	81.102		4:1-4	70
9:16-17	74.131			

Ezek			14:2	56
37:1-14	81		14:5	6*
			15:22	34*
Daniel			15:24	60*
7:13	37		15:28	58
11:40-45	80		16:14	6*
12:1-2	*21.79-80*		*17:1-8*	*110*
12:2	79*.82.132		17:3	48
			20:30s	34*
Hoseah			21:9	37
5:6	75		21:15	34*
			21:26,46	6*
Joel			21:37	60*
2:13	97*		21:39	19
			22:40	25*
Amos			24:24	57
8:10	111		24:30	37
			26:65	107
Mich			27:38	19
5:1	8		27:54	103
7:18-20	97		28:7,10	48
			28:17	48
Zech				
12:10	*35-38*.112		Mark	
			1:9-11	113
Matt			1:10	117
3:13-17	113		1:11	115.117
3:16	117		1:19,29	24*
3:17	104.113*.115		3:17	24*
4:3.6	104		4:14	92
5:17	25		4:41	57
7:12	25*		5:34	58
7:22	56		5:37	26*
7:24,26	33		6:2,5	56
8:5-13	43		6:2b	115
8:12	19		6:14	56
9:22	58		6:15	6*
9:27	34*		9:2-8	110
9:29	58		9:2	26*
10:40	60*		9:39	56
11:4-5	57		10:35,41	26*
11:13	25*		10:45	126
11:20-23	56		10:52	58
12:18	122*		11:10	37
12:23	34*		12:2	60*
12:38-39	56		12:8	19
13:48	19		12:18	113*
13:54	115		13:3	26*
13:54,58	56		13:22	57

14:33	26*	22:3	19*
14:41	51	22:43	48
14:64	107	22:53	19*
15:27	19	22:67	107
15:39	103	22:70	107
16:12,14	48*	23:8	60
		23:33	19
Luke		23:47	103
1:11	48	24:12	47.47*
1:23	116*	24:19	6*
1:34	125*	24:27	26*
1:35	116	24:34	48
2:40-52	116	24:36-39	47
3:21-22	113	24:41-43	47
3:22	117	24:41	47
3:22b	115	24:44	25*
4:1-2	114		
4:3,9	104	John	
4:13	19*	*1:1-18*	*85ss*
4:13-29	115	1:1-14	108
4:43	60*	1:1-13	141
5:1-11	47	1:1-2	72.122.131
6:46	33	1:1	94.98.125
7:1-10	43	1:1ab,3	85-87
7:9-10	58	1:3-5	72
7:11-16	10	1:4a	88
7:12	108	1:6	60
7:16	6*	1:7	24.25.60
7:21-23	57	1:9,15	61*
7:39	27	1:12-13	92
7:50	58	*1:13*	*117*
8:11-15	92	*1:14-18*	*94ss.108s.*110s
8:42	108	1:14	85.95.96.110-111.114.
8:48	58		131
9:19	6*	1:14,18	99*
9:28-36	110	1:17	96.98.133
9:32	110	1:18	95.95*.109.125
9:38	108	1:19–2:11	23
10:13	56	*1:19-51*	*23*
10:18	18.19	1:19-34	29
13:28	19	1:19.21	127
14:35	19	*1:20-21*	*29*
16:16	25*	*1:21-22*	*8*
16:29,31	26*	1:21	36.67
17:19	58	1:25	127
18:42	58	1:26,31	49
19:37	56	1:26,31-32,29	127
20:13	60	1:31	48*.49
20:15	19	1:32-34	39.117

140 BIBLICAL REFERENCES

1:32-33	49	3:28	60
1:32,34	113	4:1ss	41
1:33	60*	4:16-19	27
1:34	49	4:16-19,29	64
1:35-51	29	4:16-18	52
1:35-39	23.24	4:18	29
1:35-37	52	4:22	142
1:35	50.55	4:25	8
1:36ss	79.129	4:30	64
1:38	75.76	4:34	60*
1:39	76	4:39	64
1:41-42	28	4:41-42	64
1:41	8.32.74.75.129	4:45	54
1:41,45	29	4:46ss	42.43.53.54.58.67
1:43,49	67.127	4:46-54	127
1:43	24.67*.76	4:46a	43.47
1:45-51	38	4:46a,54a	48
1:45-49	24.26.41.55	4:46bss	42
1:45-47	28	4:46b-54	43
1:45-46	8*.28	4:48	64
1:45	6.8*.25-30.33.37	4:53	57*
	38.67.76.81.129	4:54	32.44.48.50-52.56.62
1:45,49	38.130	4:54a	46.55
1:46	54	4:54b	50*
1:49	30.37.38.94.99.102.112	5:1ss	53.54
2:1ss	34.42-43.53.55.67	5:1	53
2:1-12	127	5:14	24
2:1-11	38.53	5:19,30	61*
2:1	2	5:20,36	54
2:1b,11a	48	5:21-23,27-29	65
2:3-5	32.130	5:23,24,30,37	60*
2:5	10.33.36.37	5:24	66.83
2:6	53	5:25	89
2:11	43.44.48.48*.49.50.56.	5:27-29	82
	57.58.62.128	5:28-29	79.132
2:11a	46	5:31-47	52
2:12	42.43.54.55.127	5:36	63
2:13	43.53	5:36,38	60*
2:19-21	53	5:39	7
2:23	45.54.55.56*.57*	5:43	61*
3:2	56*.57.63	5:46-47	27.28*
3:2,19,31	61*	5:46	26.67
3:6	113	6:1ss	53
3:11-13	131	6:1-15	128
3:12-13	74	6:2	63
3:16,18	99*	6:2,14,26,30	56*
3:17ss	65	6:4	56
3:17	60	6:5-13	52
3:17,34	60*	6:7-8	24

12:48-50	*11-14*.17.65.67.130	19:37	37.38
12:48	*15*.65.82.132	20:3-10	47.47*
12:49-50	15.19.62	20:17	103.104
12:49a-50b	*17*	20:18,20,25,28	45
13:1	*20.21*.53	20:18,25	48
13:19	120	20:19-20	50
13:27,30	19	20:20	48
14:1ss	19.20.22	20:28	123.125
14:1	22	20:29	48.64
14:2-4	*21*	20:30-31	57*
14:3	75	20:30	56*
14:6	119	21:1ss	42.53.55.67
14:10-12	54	*21:1-14*	45.*46*.52.128
14:10	*16.17*.61*.62.67	21:1-4,6-8,11	50
14:11	57*	21:1,14	48*.52.127
14:21	*73*.130	21:2	52
14:24	62	21:5	47
14:27	24	21:5,9,12-13	47
14:30-31	19	21:6,8,11	46
15:3	53	21:7,12	45
15:6	19	21:9,13	46
15:22-24	67	21:10	49
15:24	54	21:14	47.50-52.61
16:12-13	132	21:14b	48*
16:28	98	21:16	45
17:2	113	21:17	51
17:3	41.*123-125*.132		
17:5	87	Acts	
17:6	19	2:3	48
17:6,8,26	67	3:22-23	6*
17:8	*17*.130	3:22	59.67
17:8,14	62	4:16,22	59
17:24	75	7:2,30	48
18:4-6	122	7:37	7*.59
18:28	22.53	8:5ss	67*
18:33	37	8:6	59
18:33,37	37	9:17	48
18:39	53	9:35,42	59
19:7	104	13:31	48
19:14	53	16:9	48
19:15-16	37	26:16	48
19:17-18	*20*.128	26:22	26*
19:18	20	28:23	25*
19:19	37		
19:25-27	38	Rom	
19:28	20	3:21	25*
19:31ss	20	9:5	123*
19:31-37	38		
19:35	38		

1 Cor			**2 Peter**	
9:1	48		1:1	123*
15:5-8	48		1:16-17	111
2 Cor			**1 John**	
12:14	51		1:2	87*
13:1	51		2:14	92
			2:18-23	125
Col			3:1.9-10	100
1:15	109*		3:14	66
3:3-4	87*		3:22	16
			4:9	99*
1 Thess			4:12	95
1:9	124		5:19	19.21
			5:20	41.*123-125*.131
1 Tim				
2:5	126		**2 John**	
2:6	126		4	40
Tit			**3 John**	
2:13-14	126		3.4	40
2:13	123*.126			
2:14	126		**Rev**	
			1:7	37
Heb			11:19	48
11:17	108		12:1,3	48
			12:9	18.19
Jas				
1:16-22	93			
1 Peter				
1:22–2:1	93			
1:25	93			

INDEX OF AUTHORS CITED